PEACE BOOK

DAVE NOBLE

Vietnam: father and child

Writers and Readers Publishing Cooperative
14 Talacre Road, London NW5 3PE
First published 1977 ©Copyright Dave Noble, 1977
Illustration research by Diana Phillips and Christine Vincent
Designed by Arthur Lockwood
for Ikon, 25 St Pancras Way, London NW1
Photoset by Red Lion Setters, Holborn, London.
Made and printed in Great Britain by The Garden City Press

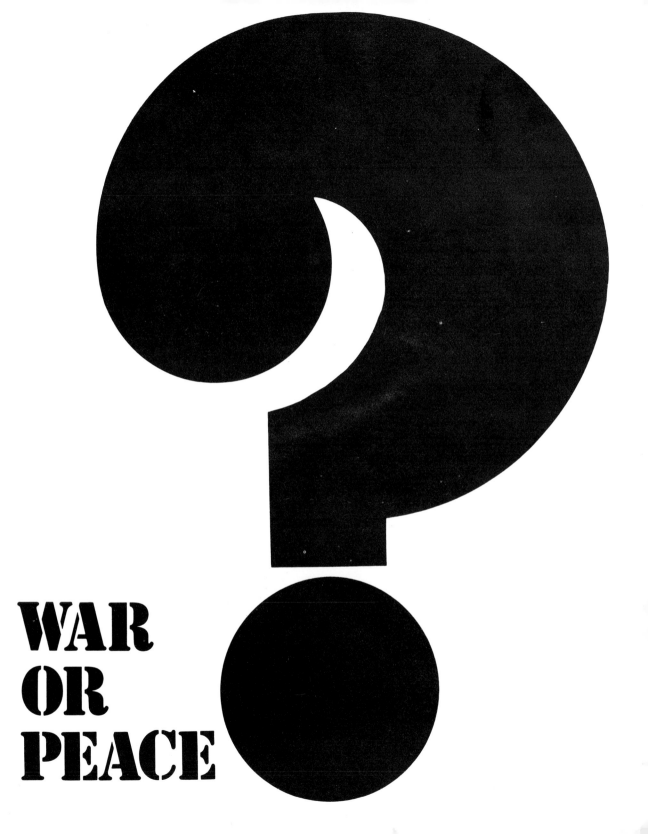

WAR
OR
PEACE

THE WAR &

Vietnam: soldiers resting

Writers
and Readers
Publishing
Cooperative

CONTENTS

1 BEFORE THE STORM

'... there is no parallel in nature to our savage treatment of each other'.

Anthony Storr, *Human Aggression*

Chinese girls in bayonet practice

HOLIDAY SPECIAL

WAR PICTURE LIBRARY 20p

ON SALE NOW!

Fighting the old battles. Collecting Nazi mementoes, making model planes or playing with the real thing.

'Don't tell me __ it's another programme about the Second World War'

It is unpleasant to think the unthinkable. But odds are now one in three that a nuclear weapon will be detonated before 1984, possibly triggering the final holocaust.

The prediction comes from Bernard Feld, a sober-minded expert on disarmament negotiations at the Massachusetts Institute of Technology. His views are echoed by other doomsday spotters. A group of five experts at a Harvard University symposium concluded that nuclear war in some form is likely before the end of the century, and that it will probably occur as the direct result of a proliferation of nuclear power and weaponry. Thomas Schelling, a Harvard political economy professor and arms control expert, predicted: 'We will not be able to regulate nuclear weapons around the world in 1999 any better than we can control the Saturday-night special, heroin, or pornography today.'

We have been lulled by a generation of peace in Europe and America, a spurious lull cosmetized by unprecedented affluence in industrialised nations and gross poverty everywhere else. The nuclear arms race roars ahead despite so-called arms 'control' agreements, while Western and Eastern bloc nations fatten on gigantic arms sales to the poorer countries. America and Russia now have enough silo-stored nuclear weapons to blast each other apart ten times over, with quantity and quality improving each year.

Prospective parents should think again before ushering children onto our nuclear-mined planet. Prudent investors should consider the relevance of life insurance and retirement schemes — retirement for everyone may occur prematurely. Only the push of buttons and whirl of computer reels are required to zap nations from the map.

9

But Suicide Lane is studded not only with nuclear weapons, but with spiralling expenditure on sophisticated non-nuclear weaponry. Non-nuclear war has become more common in many poor nations than a daily piece of bread. The non-Western world since 1945 has been flooded with armaments and even troops from industrialised nations. The fighting has greatly stimulated weapons technology, and high profit armaments industries intimately linked with national governments churn out frighteningly effective equipment.

Our fateful and possibly final planetary journey has not been halted by one single pure act of disarmament since the United Nations was established in 1945. Nuclear weapons have been banned from areas like Antarctica and Outer Space, but the military have scant interest in these bleak regions.

In the late 1950s and 1960s there was an outcry against testing of nuclear weapons in the atmosphere. Many ordinary people, black and white, yellow and brown, rich and poor, joined ranks to protest against radioactive contamination of Spaceship Earth. The outcry was heeded. The Soviet, American and British governments were compelled to perfect underground testing. In 1975 France announced it would abandon above-ground tests in the Pacific, a decision prompted by an international storm of protest.

Our leaders have failed us. The professional negotiators turn an ever more cynical ear to demands that moves at least be started towards disarmament. Time is running out. The 'decision-makers' have had 30 years to make their decisions. All they seem to have done is drag the planet deeper into the mire of militarism, tension and war.

'Decision-makers' fail when the public is passive. As we move closer to the ultimate nuclear nightmare, only massive public protests can arrest the headlong plunge down Suicide Lane.

The lives we save may be our own.

A radar operations centre, part of a NATO defence project costing £110 million.

A surface to air missile is put through its paces.

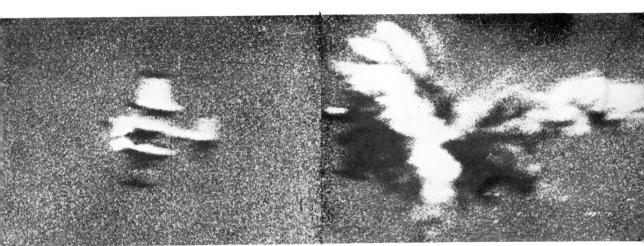

2 A WAR A DAY

'It is quite untrue that if one wishes for peace one should prepare for war; but if one wishes for peace one should understand war.'

B.H. Liddell Hart, *Aggression*

Despite a fundamental horror of violence, the inhabitants of this planet have busily slaughtered one another for tens of thousands of years. In the past, conflict has been caused by man's search for fertile land, for greater power or greater wealth. Men have also fought to achieve freedom from oppression, or for what they have described as religious reasons.

Warfare engaging hundreds of millions of people is a comparatively recent development. In these days, hardly a moment goes by without a war being waged somewhere.

Between 1945 and 1969, some 97 wars were fought, in 59 countries. They ranged from guerrilla warfare in Cuba and Indochina to 'conventional' conflicts in Korea, Biafra and the Middle East. Some, like the Kurdish uprising in Iraq and the strife in Bangladesh, could be classified as wars of independence. Conflict between Catholic and Protestant in Northern Ireland and between Catholic and Moslem in the Philippines had religious undertones, although social and economic reasons were paramount. Two Latin American countries even went to war because of a football match!

Conflict in Beirut, an old woman being escorted away from the fighting.

An acoustic beacon in an infra-sound research laboratory: how long will science fiction still seem fantastic?

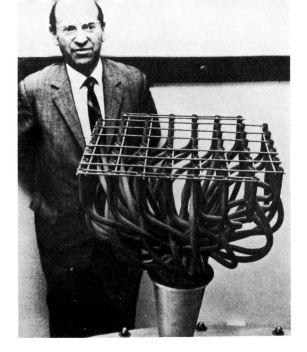

Apart from all the suffering, these modern wars have one thing in common: the weaponry is more advanced and effective than ever. General W.C. Westmoreland, former Chief of Staff of the United States Army, described his 'vision' of the battle of the future, after touring Vietnam in 1969.

The general said that before long enemy forces will be tracked down and 'targeted' almost instantaneously with the help of data links, computer assisted intelligence evaluation, and automated fire control. The need for large forces to oppose the enemy will be less important, because sensor devices will stalk down the enemy, 'with first round kill probabilities approaching certainty. . . .'

On tomorrow's automated battlefield, he continued, 'we can destroy anything we locate through instant communications and the almost instantaneous application of high lethal firepower. . . . Currently we have hundreds of surveillance, target acquisition, night observation and information processing systems either in being, in development or in engineering. With cooperative effort, no more than 10 years should separate us from the automated battlefield.'

New weapons for old

We already have the means to blow up and incinerate people on a mass scale, devastate forests and chemically destroy crops and all wildlife. But now military scientists are researching 'devices' like sound cannon, which use infrasound waves to cause reduced vision or blindness, a sense of suffocation, nausea and dizziness. Another weapon in the works produces blinding light flashes, which can lead to permanent eye damage and bring on epileptic fits.

Scientists in several countries are researching ways to produce earthquakes by using nuclear bombs or other high explosives. Tampering with the earth's delicate crust could result in floods and landslides to hinder an enemy. Even during the Vietnam War the Americans induced rain by seeding clouds with chemicals to make roads or terrain impassable. Environmental warfare in Vietnam included razing of forests by firebombs and defoliants, ruination of fields and crops by chemicals sprayed from the air, and removal of villages by giant bulldozers. The use of such techniques could result in disastrous ecological changes: the chemicals which defoliated forests and killed plants may have caused deformed babies in Vietnam.

From 1961 to 1971 the American Air Force dropped about 120 million pounds (55 million kg) of herbicides, and about a tenth of South Vietnam's land area was sprayed with far stronger chemical agents.

Although it cannot be proved conclusively, several scientific studies have indicated that dioxin, a toxic agent found in one of the herbicides, can cause liver damage, stillbirths, fatal abnormalities, genetic changes and cancer.

A study by the American National Academy of Sciences concludes that herbicidal use in Vietnam caused damage to the ecology that would take a hundred years to heal. Inland tropical forests were extensively damaged, and 36 per cent of the nation's mangrove forests along the coast perished. In these areas the delicate balance of nature was seriously disturbed, and may never recover. The study discounted claims by the military that herbicides did not endanger human life. The Academy quoted allegations that several children died after crops in their district were sprayed by planes 'spraying smoke,' as villagers put it. Adults said they suffered abdominal pains, intense coughing and rashes which looked like giant insect bites.

The Americans were not the first to use defoliants in military operations. This dubious honour goes to the British, who used them in the mid-1950s while warring in colonial Malaya with insurgents. Vietnam, however, proved a perfect testing ground for environmental warfare. Scientists were not content to strip trees and shrubs of leaves. Efforts were also made to destroy forests. Between 1965 and 1969 they tried to ignite large scale forest fires or stoke fires already blazing. Planes dropped huge quantities of incendiary bombs in abortive efforts to create firestorms. The results of these experiments remain a secret, though evidence indicates they were unsuccessful because of Vietnam's perenially wet climate.

The scientific mind gained greater satisfaction from the damage caused by 'land-clearing' programmes. Huge bulldozers and tractors equipped with special blades levelled more than 1,000 acres of forest a day at one stage of the war. Another forest removal programme involved a 7½ ton bomb called the 'Daisy Cutter.' Its detonation created an instant clearing three to four acres in size, and the blast wave travelled outwards for about 1,300 feet, killing anything in its path. The super-bomb was originally designed to create a clearing for helicopter landing pads, but American military planners were nothing if not versatile.

'The local ecological impact of removing all the vegetation and exposing the soil on thousands of acres at a time is phenomenal,' said Professor Arthur Westing, an American expert on environmental war. He said that soil without vegetation immediately succumbs to massive erosion, particularly in hilly terrain, while the soil which remains loses most of its soluble minerals. Sooner or later the cleared areas are invaded by weeds. 'This means of area denial (to an enemy force) has thus served to convert large tracts of Indochina into what might be referred to as a semi-permanent green desert,' Dr Westing stated.

Petrified forest:
Vietnam after defoliation.

Chemical warfare

Chemical and biological weapons are nothing new, of course, and the main problem prohibiting widespread use is the fact that they are difficult to control. The 1899 Hague Peace Conference adopted a resolution banning use of asphyxiating gases. But generals in World War I chose to ignore or deliberately misinterpret the 'ban,' and both sides attempted relatively widescale use of gas weapons. Initially they deployed gas resembling tear gas, but by the end of the war toxic substances such as mustard gas were being used to kill or incapacitate. The difficulty was that the gas might be blown by a shift of wind onto your own side.

WILLS'S CIGARETTES

THE CIVILIAN RESPIRATOR—
HOW TO REMOVE IT

5'S CIGARETTES

RUBBER CLOTHING

Protection from gas attack: during World War I (left); World War II (above); and (right) waiting for World War III?

In 1925 over 90 countries ratified an agreement to ban wartime use of asphyxiating, poisonous or similar gases, as well as bacteriological weapons. But the temptations remained. Two decades later the Italians used gas against civilians in Ethiopia, reportedly fitting special tanks to aircraft which enabled gas to be sprayed over vast areas of countryside onto unprepared and unprotected civilians. The aircraft flew in formations of up to 18 to ensure a thick blanket of the stuff. The Japanese reportedly used chemical weapons when they invaded China in 1937. And about 600 Chinese soldiers were said to have died in 1941 after being bombarded with gas shells.

Since World War II there have been many unsubstantiated reports of gas used in war zones, including Algeria in 1957 during the war of independence against France, the Yemen during the 1963-7 civil war, and Iraq in operations against Kurdish guerrillas. During the Indochina War there were frequent outcries about use of chemical weapons. The Americans admitted using irritant gases such as tear gas or nausea gas, but stated that this did not violate international agreements.

Among the most deadly nerve gases now available are VX, Sarin and Soman, which can be inhaled directly or absorbed through the skin. Attacking the nervous system, death occurs within minutes. The effects, in the following order, start with tightness of chest, and then reduced vision, drooling and excessive sweating, vomiting, cramps, involuntary defecation and urination, twitching, coma, convulsion and finally death.

Biological or germ warfare has always been regarded with revulsion. It is only a remote possibility at the present time, because it presents too many production, storage and delivery problems to be a convenient alternative to conventional or nuclear war. In medieval times it was quite common to toss dead bodies into wells to make the water either unfit for consumption or to create infectious diseases. Corpses of diseased men or animals were also thrown into besieged cities to spread infection. As late as World War I the Germans allegedly tried to kill enemy horses by exposing them to a highly contagious disease called glanders. There were reports during World War II that the Japanese used germ warfare by introducing cholera in parts of central China in 1942. Germs were allegedly scattered from airplanes.

Gruinard Island — not fit to live on for a century.

GRUINARD ISLAND
THIS ISLAND IS
GOVERNMENT PROPERTY
UNDER EXPERIMENT
THE GROUND IS CONTAMINATED
WITH ANTHRAX AND DANGEROUS.
LANDING IS PROHIBITED
BY ORDER 19

But it is difficult to find supporting evidence, chiefly because germs are difficult to trace, and hard to control. The British discovered this after bombarding the tiny Gruinard Island off the Scottish coast with anthrax spores, as part of a grisly experiment. Tests carried out afterwards reportedly showed that the island would be uninhabitable for perhaps 100 years.

Concern about germ warfare has thus been so widespread that the only treaty signed in the past few decades involving 'disarmament' is a 1972 international convention banning the development, production and stockpiling of biological weapons, and requiring destruction of existing stocks.

Unseeing weapons

Weapons technology has 'advanced' so much in the past decade that we are rapidly approaching General Westmoreland's automated vision. His battlefield is nearly a reality: radar and specialised television systems permit the modern warrior to aim at a target he cannot see with his own eyes. Even small missiles have built-in homing devices, such as a heat-seeking unit, allowing them to reach targets more accurately. Until World War II targets were generally located visually, but as the war progressed radar became more widespread. Nowadays, highly sensitive sensors can not only pick up troop movements, but in some cases identify what is causing them. Once movement is registered, the sensor immediately flashes the information to a control centre, which is situated many miles away, or in a plane circling above the site. Use of sensors allows an army to keep an 'eye' on a specific area where enemy movements are suspected. By stringing the sensors over a broad area an army can thus follow enemy movements by remote control and then fire weapons at targets indicated by sensors.

Sensors are not completely perfected. It is possible to hamper them once you know where they are. Dummy vehicles can be sent across roads where sensors are suspected, thus causing shelling of the area. Once the barrage ends, troop movements can begin. In Vietnam the Americans used a sensor known as a 'people sniffer', which reacted to bodily chemicals. Vietnamese guerrillas foiled the sniffers by dangling bags of urine around them, which upset the sensors' chemicals.

Information gathered by sensors is transmitted to the control centre's computer, which is

An Israeli Phantom, capable of holding more than 8 tons of bombs, missiles and rockets.

capable of handling about 40,000 reports at once. Sensors planted along the so-called Ho Chi Minh Trail in Laos kept an eye on supplies being moved to guerrillas in South Vietnam, and the information digested by the computer provided a sketch on a screen of the area concerned, showing the movements occurring. The U.S. Air Force frequently carried out air strikes as a direct result of this information.

Until now the final decision for action against a target spotted by sensors has remained in the hands of human beings at control centres. But, as General Westmoreland indicated, the day is coming when a computer will be 'allowed' to react automatically to information received by sensors, either by issuing orders to military units or setting into motion a missile strike. But present sensor technology cannot guarantee whether troops or simply civilians are in the target area.

Reaction to these movements at present takes the form of missile or artillery bombardment or air strikes by fighter-bombers, helicopter gunships or remote controlled unmanned aircraft. In Indochina the Americans used the F4 Phantom (a two seat, long-range, all-weather, missile-bearing jet fighter) equipped with a special computer which automatically guided the plane to the target, based upon information received from sensors. The bomb load was automatically released by the computer. Computers were also fitted onto helicopter gunships, which flew the crafts automatically and aimed and fired their 40mm cannon. These cannon can spew up to 250 rounds per minute up to a range of 3,000 feet (1,000 metres) once the target has been spotted by sensors.

An American B-52 unloads a Short-Range Attack Missile [SRAM].

The modern warplane itself is a highly complicated piece of machinery designed to be highly adaptable. The multi-role aircraft can be a fighter, supporting ground troops or installations, or a fighter-bomber which conducts air strikes against targets miles from base. Reconnaissance, weapons delivery, interception and submarine hunting are also possible. But it cannot replace the modern bomber, which can carry a much higher payload of destruction. Bombs dropped from high-flying bombers can be distributed over a fairly wide area, and intensive bombing can wreak terrible damage. A missile called SRAM (Short Range Attack Missile), an American invention, has also given the bomber a new lease of life in a nuclear war. It is designed to knock out radar installations and anti-aircraft positions along the flight path leading to the target, creating a hazard-free trail. The American B52 bombers can carry up to 24 SRAMs, each packing a sizeable nuclear warhead, in addition to the usual quantity of bombs.

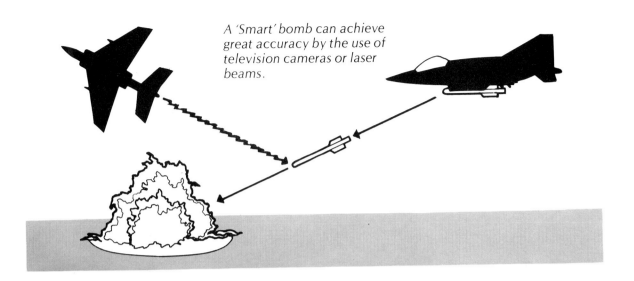

A 'Smart' bomb can achieve great accuracy by the use of television cameras or laser beams.

But warplanes can be stopped. Egyptian missiles took a heavy toll of Israeli aircraft during the 1974 Middle East ('Yom Kippur') War. The Israelis lost heavily in the opening stages of fighting as they attempted to stem the Egyptian advance into the Sinai and the Syrian assaults on the Golan Heights. In one day, for example, about 30 Israeli bombers were believed shot down by Soviet-built missiles. However, the Israelis learned how to evade surface-to-air missiles. They discovered that certain Russian-built missiles can only be fired at a bomber after the plane has passed the site, and it can be thwarted if the pilot releases a flare which fools the missile's guidance system, which is taught to respond to heat.

Military leaders are also focussing attention upon remote-controlled attack planes armed with bombs or missiles. They are guided by an operator seated miles away, who follows television pictures transmitted from a camera in the nose of the plane. He directs the flight from a ground control centre, or from a centre aboard another plane in flight. Tests have shown that a trained operator can guide the unmanned plane as though he were in the cockpit.

The unmanned attack plane has several advantages. It is smaller and therefore cheaper, costing about $300,000 compared with $15 million for the conventional bomber. It has good reconnaissance potential due to its small size, which makes it difficult to spot with the naked eye. It has a specially designed body which is difficult to pick up on radar screens, and if the plane should be downed, there is no highly trained pilot to be killed or captured.

The main disadvantages of a remote-controlled aircraft are its limited endurance and the restricted field of vision provided by the camera. Both problems are being surmounted rapidly. The latest remote-controlled planes are said to be able to remain in the air for up to twenty-four hours at a time, while vision has been improved by placing cameras along the fuselage as well as in the nose.

Bombs and missiles are being equipped with built-in automatic or guided homing devices. Some 'smart' missiles can find their way to a target without further help, even if the target takes evasive action. The homing system can be an infra-red seeking device which 'guides' the missile towards heat sources, such as the hot exhaust of aircraft engines. Or there could be a radar seeking device which homes in on radar stations above ground. These missiles were used by the Americans in Indochina, and by both sides during the 1974 Middle East War.

Fletchettes [actual size]

Bombs dropped from planes can be guided towards a target. The American 'Walleye' bomb, for instance, has a television camera mounted in its nose. An image of the target area seen by the television camera is displayed on a monitor screen in the aircraft. The bomb aimer is able to 'lock' the bomb onto a specific target, and the accuracy of this method is believed to be very high.

Precision bombing is irrelevant when the exact location of the target is not known. In that event, a large bomb can be used to devastate a wide area, as well as bombs which explode into hundreds and even thousands of tiny pieces flying in all directions, damaging, killing or maiming. Cluster bombs carry fragmentation warheads, incendiary or chemical agents. In modern wars about 70 per cent of military casualties and 80 per cent of civilian casualties have been caused by fragmentation and blast weapons. A typical cluster bomb consists of a large hollow container filled with 600 or so small 'bomblets.' Dropped from the air, the container splits open at a pre-determined height, scattering the bomblets over an area up to 3,000 feet (1,000 metres) long and 900 feet (300 metres) wide. Each bomblet has been built so that when it detonates in the air or hits the ground, hundreds of small pieces of jagged metal are sent flying in all directions. Some bomblets may contain a high number of pellets resembling ball bearings, or incendiaries or nerve gases. The effects are staggering. These weapons are used against human targets, although the shrapnel may also puncture tyres, fuel tanks and radiators of unprotected vehicles. Other versions have been developed with time fuses aimed at hindering rescue operations.

'Small and nasty'

Variations on the theme are bullets, rockets and shells containing up to 5,000 small darts called 'fletchettes'. It is reported that one well-aimed artillery round containing fletchettes could kill hundreds of troops massing for attack. Fletchettes are tiny metal darts about one inch long, with fins on the tail which rip people open like a machine drill. Several fletchettes are encased in a plastic container which is fixed onto a powder cartridge and then loaded into the breech of a rifle or more ambitious launching device. After leaving the barrel, the container splits apart, leaving the fletchettes to continue at high velocity all around an area. They tend to tumble upon impact, inflicting nasty and usually fatal wounds.

Asked about medical treatment for a person hit by several fletchettes, an American army officer reportedly said: 'Don't kid yourself. It's not a job for a surgeon but for graves registration.' A 20-fletchette shotgun cartridge is already in use, and scientists are working out how to cram more than 30 into a single plastic bullet.

Another nasty way to die is provided by a fuel air explosive, which can kill or wound concealed troops and destroy land mines, booby traps and light vehicles. It consists of a canister dropped from a plane or fired from a cannon which breaks open at a certain height, dispensing a vaporized cloud of chemicals. The cloud is then ignited by a detonator which causes an explosion, and the blast effects are far more effective than standard explosives. During a conventional artillery or aerial bombardment, a human being can be protected from blast waves by trees or trenches. But the fuel air explosive sends its blast shock waves not only outwards but also downwards, towards the ground. Human beings are left defenceless.

German Flame throwers during World War I.

Another highly indiscriminate device is napalm, and similar incendiary weapons, which cause the most frightening and severe burns (believed by doctors to constitute the most severe trauma to which the human body can be subjected). In 1932 the League of Nations resolved that the gross cruelty caused by incendiary weapons like napalm cannot be regarded as necessary from a military standpoint.

Nonetheless, napalm and similar weapons have been used extensively against armies and civilians, although they are intended for use against metals and substances far more robust than the human frame. Victims of serious napalm burns, moreover, do not necessarily die immediately. They may linger on in excruciating pain for hours, days, sometimes weeks. Death usually results from loss of fluids, from infection or from the extra strain placed on the heart, kidney or lungs.

Incendiary weapons are nothing new. The ancient Spartans used a mixture of pitch and sulphur in the fourth century B.C. to burn down cities, and petroleum or naptha was added later on to improve the mixture. During the seventh century incendiary weapons were invented which could be spurted from special siphons — the flame throwers of the day.

25

A Vietnamese girl tears off her burning clothes after an accidental napalm raid.

During World War II an estimated four-fifths of fire damage in Britain resulted from incendiary bombing, and the situation was much the same in Germany. Air raids on Japanese cities, at that time built mostly of wood, consisted of incendiary bomb attacks. Over 83,000 people died in one incendiary air raid in Tokyo in March 1945. Nearly 41,000 more were injured in the raid, and about one million became homeless.

Napalm, the most common incendiary, is a highly flammable jelly made from aviation fuel and certain chemicals, which cause it to stick to its target. In the mid-1960s a new thickener — polystyrene — was added which made napalm even more adhesive. The wounds are horrific. Even if victims survive initial burns, they will be badly scarred or crippled for life. Skin cancer is also much more likely to develop in scars caused by burns than in normal skin. White phosphorous, another incendiary agent, has been used in grenades, smoke bombs, artillery shells and other weapons. It is difficult to extinguish, and may continue to burn even after entry into a human body. Unless dealt with immediately, it can go on burning for hours and even days. It is also highly poisonous. If phosphorous remains embedded in the skin for any length of time it can cause lethal damage to the liver, heart and kidneys.

*A rubber bullet —
for crowd control.*

The military have argued that incendiary weapons like napalm are not as bad as they would appear. Efforts have been made to show that soldiers run little risk of death. One study said that when a group of 54 American soldiers in South Vietnam were inadvertently bombed with napalm, 'only' four died. But the soldiers were trained to deal with incendiary attacks and equipped with anti-napalm instruments. They received advanced medical care within minutes, which greatly increased chances of survival. Nothing is said about untrained and unprepared civilians, suddenly confronted with a fire storm of searing, sticky napalm. You cannot brush it away, as it sticks to your hands.

Many have professed disgust at the use of weapons causing such terrible injuries. But even modern rifle and pistol bullets cause the same frightful wounds inflicted by dum-dum bullets, which were banned as 'inhumane' in 1899. A high velocity bullet fired from the modern rifle tends to be highly unstable as it enters a man's body. It generates powerful shock waves which open a gaping hole far bigger than the bullet itself. According to a report published in 1973 by the Swedish Defence Ministry, high-velocity modern bullets produce an explosive effect upon impact similar to the dum-dum, inflicting 'grossly inhumane damage to humans.' An ugly recent innovation is 'salvo squeezebore' — a round fired from a hand-held weapon such as a semi-automatic rifle. Each round consists of a cartridge of small, high velocity bullets, which fan out as they speed towards the target.

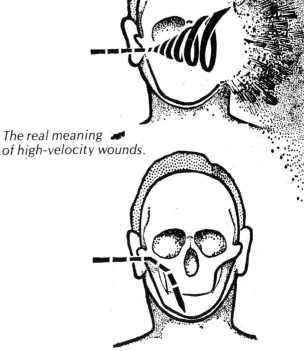

*The real meaning
of high-velocity wounds.*

27

Tanks and missiles

Since World War II the military have had to reconsider how modern warfare should be waged. In Vietnam, for instance, it was proved that a well-organised guerrilla force could successfully take on a 'Super Power', so long as it avoided conventional battles. If a guerrilla force has general support from the populace and active economic and military assistance from external sources, its chances of victory are very good. The Vietnam War showed that to wage war seriously against guerrillas meant using techniques which will eventually antagonise the population — the very reverse, presumably, of what is intended. The modern army fighting a guerrilla force, as

Vietnam showed, is forced to resort to so-called 'search and destroy' and 'seize and hold' operations against the local population. In Vietnam helicopter gunships would patrol areas where civilians were banned. But civilians did not always know this. Any movement provoked immediate attack. Add to this the terrible damage wreaked by heavy bombardment of guerrilla-controlled areas, and it becomes understandable why the Americans failed to win the 'hearts and minds' of the Vietnamese.

The Indochina War, along with the 1974 Middle East conflict, also demonstrated the power and the importance of missiles, which has meant that several blueprints for modern wars have been quietly scrapped. In the 1974 war, Egypt and Syria, on the one hand, and Israel on the other, together used more than 4,000 tanks and over 2,000 aircraft. When the war ended 18 days later nearly 500 planes had been shot down and almost 2,000 tanks knocked out of action by missiles. Heavy equipment losses contributed to the millions of dollars spent by both sides during the fighting. Israel alone spent an estimated $175,000 a minute in a conflict where extensive and effective use was made not only of air-to-air and air-to-surface missiles, but also of surface-to-air and anti-tank missiles. Tanks were lost at the rate of one every 16 minutes, while one fighter jet was shot down every hour.

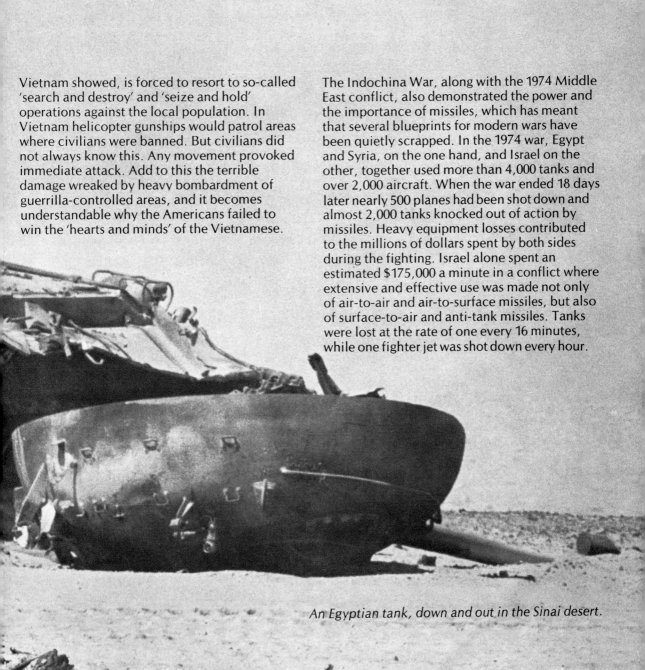

An Egyptian tank, down and out in the Sinai desert.

Inside a chieftain tank.

Before this war, the classic way to stop a tank was to use an armour piercing shell, which penetrated up to eight inches of armour plate steel, and then fragmented inside the tank, sending lethal fragments flying in all directions, and hitting crew and vital components. Even if the shell did not penetrate, it could still cause damage. The new option is called HEAT, a high explosive anti-tank warhead fitted to a missile, fired from the shoulder by an infantryman from a bazooka-like launcher. When a tank is struck by the warhead a jet of high velocity copper particles slice almost instantaneously through the steel armour. Within the tank, bits of its walling are impacted and fly about in the crew enclosure. Meantime, the jet of particles continues to slice through anything in the way, and because of its high temperature it sets alight any inflammable material.

Arab armies were equipped with a Soviet built anti-tank missile known in the West as the 'Sagger.' It is guided towards the target by a control wire manipulated by the firer. The missile can be fired from either an armoured car or by an infantryman. A fine wire trails from a reel attached to the missile. Using a special optical sight, the gunner guides the missile onto the target. It is said to be accurate and effective against tanks up to 9,000 feet (3,000 metres) away. Another anti-tank missile used effectively by Arabs in 1974 was the Soviet-built RPG7 rocket launcher, which fires a small unguided missile. It proved devastating in close-in fighting and ambushes against armoured

Shouldering the SAM-7 missile.

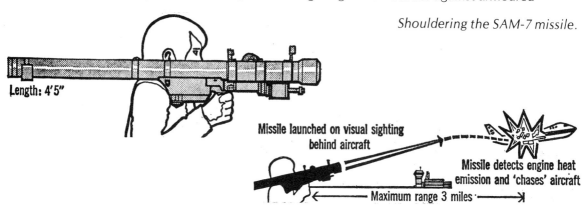

Length: 4'5"

Missile launched on visual sighting behind aircraft

Missile detects engine heat emission and 'chases' aircraft

Maximum range 3 miles

vehicles. This ultimate anti-tank missile is fully automatic, of course. Like the American surface-to-air missiles, it carries a small television camera in its nose, linked to a computer programmed to 'recognise' a tank and then zero in on the missile on the target.

At the start of the Yom Kippur War, the Israelis made little use of missiles, but relied upon conventional tank gunnery against other tanks and armoured targets. However, the highly effective use of small missiles by Arabs apparently persuaded the United States — Israel's chief military supplier — to provide them with anti-tank missiles towards the end of the war.

Some have interpreted the lessons from this war as indicating that the days of the tank are numbered. Not everyone would agree. New types of armour, it is pointed out, are being developed which provide protection against a strike from anything except an enormous missile. In addition, modern tanks are relatively light and very fast. The main battle tactic employed is to 'shoot and scoot.' A tank might appear over the brow of a hill, sight a target, fire three shots and then depart as rapidly as possible to avoid retaliation. As one Israeli tank commander recalled: 'If you have not hit the enemy by the third shot, you had better get moving'.

Such tactics tend to limit missiles as tank weapons. An ordinary tank cannon can usually be fired on the move, admittedly with limited accuracy. But a missile usually needs to be guided onto the target in order to be a hundred per cent effective. To help get around this problem, some tanks are now equipped with a dual-purpose gun, which will fire either a missile or a shell.

How the Israelis were wounded in the 1973 war.

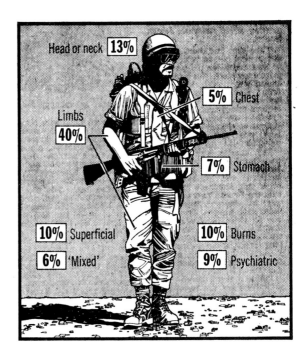

The role of the infantryman is changing rapidly. Use of missiles in the Yom Kippur War showed that the foot soldier, equipped with a light-weight, easy-to-use missile which can be fired from a small launcher, has the ability to hinder movement and air-power. His greatest hazard consists not of bullets but shrapnel. This results from increasing use of missiles, and the trend towards manufacturing shell and rocket casings which send hundreds of small fragments spraying upon impact. A study published by the Israeli Medical Association shortly after the war stated that most injuries treated resulted from shrapnel wounds. Many of the wounded had suffered from varying degrees of eye injuries. Soldiers may have to wear special splinter-proof eye or face masks in future.

31

All at sea

In the age of intercontinental missiles, it is sometimes forgotten that sea power still plays a vital role in defence policies of many nations. But more than two-thirds of the globe's surface is water, and the commercial importance of the sea is obvious.

In recent years the United States and the Soviet Union have greatly increased the offensive fire power of their fleets. American vessels which were once armed with missiles intended primarily for defence against attacking aircraft are now being provided with the powerful surface-to-surface Harpoon missiles. They can carry a powerful warhead for up to sixty miles. The modern destroyer bears little resemblance to even those dating back twenty years. Packed with electronic equipment, their armaments are automatically operated and fired, and use radar and remote-control television systems to direct fire against surface and air targets.

The centrepiece of the modern navy is the nuclear submarine. It can travel great distances, and remain submerged for long periods. The nuclear submarine has been called one of the most perfect weapons of war. Gliding 3,000 feet below the surface, it is nearly indestructible, and can strike at almost any point on the globe. The American Poseidon nuclear submarine can remain submerged for eight weeks at a time, has a speed of about twenty-five knots, and carries two full crews so that it is fully manned on a twenty-four hour basis. Each is armed with sixteen powerful nuclear missiles. The United States and the Soviet Union each have more than forty strategic submarines prowling the depths.

A Polaris commander four-square on his submarine's deck. Below: open doors show where the missiles are housed.

The American Navy is building a giant nuclear submarine called the Trident, which will ultimately replace the Poseidon and Polaris submarines now in service. The Trident will weigh twice as much as the current Poseidon — about 19,000 tons in all — and will be about 540 feet (179 metres) long. It will be much faster than any submarine now in existence, with a planned top speed of about forty knots, and carry bigger and more powerful missiles. A special missile is being developed for it, which would have a range of over nine thousand kilometres.

Because of the submarine's relative invulnerability, their missiles until now have been viewed as a defensive and deterrent force, to be deployed in a retaliatory attack against an opponent's cities or industrial centres. But the submarine missile is not accurate enough to attack a 'hard' target, such as an underground missile silo, which requires a nearly direct hit to be put out of action. This ability to score an almost direct hit on silos is generally called 'counterforce'. However, submarine-launched missiles are becoming more accurate, and

within a decade should have a counterforce role. It other words, the nuclear submarine, equipped with missiles which can be fired from beneath the surface, would have a strategic and offensive role, rather than a purely defensive one: their targets would be land-based.

Many believe that the submarine is rapidly becoming more important than land-based underground missile silos. A silo position, after all, is fixed, while a submarine is on the move all the time, and therefore very difficult to spot. This fact has resulted in new thinking about antisubmarine warfare. Previously, it was aimed at stopping submarines from attacking ships. Now the problem is finding them — they are then relatively easy to destroy.

The main detection device is sonar, either passive or active. Passive sonar listens for noises emanating from a submarine, such as engine noise or water disturbance from the hull. Active sonar send out a series of sound pulses, which bounce back to the operator after hitting a solid object. The well-trained sonar operator can often tell the nature of the object by the intensity of the sound bouncing back.

But sonar has its limitations. It is rather like looking for the needle in the proverbial haystack. You have to suspect something is in the area to start sonar soundings, and you have to cover a wide area to have any hope of tracking down the submarine. Sonar also has a limited range, is affected by water temperatures and, because its sound waves are audible, lets the submarine know that it is being hunted. And this, of course, leads to evasive action.

Another means of tracking a submarine is to search the depths with radar. Here, again, there are limitations. A submarine lying still on the seabed stands a good chance of not being picked up by radar, as it will often blend in with the ocean floor.

A sort of ultimate madness is conjured up by these silvery and deadly creatures prowling the depths of the world's oceans for months on end, hard to spot, each with enough of a nuclear punch to obliterate many cities and cause incredible mass destruction. It is said that mankind originated from the sea: it seems our end could come bursting from its depths.

Holes in the sky
to deep fry mankind

One fond military dream is to harness the burning rays of the sun to deep-fry human beings and destroy crops and cattle. It sounds like science fiction. But the scientific know-how exists.

Life on this planet is protected from the deadly ultraviolet radiation of sun rays because of a thin layer of ozone. This is a form of oxygen, a band lying between an altitude of 15 and 20 kilometres, which absorbs ultraviolet radiation. Total destruction of all forms of exposed life would result if the planet was exposed to the full force of ultraviolet rays.

Ozone is replaced daily. But scientists have discovered that it would be relatively simple to punch a temporary small 'hole' in the ozone band by exploding a nuclear bomb near it. Ozone in the region would be destroyed by oxides of nitrogen emanating from the explosion. Probably other means can be found to punch holes in the sky.

... or holes in the ground to swallow us all

Scientists are devising ways to set artificially into motion an earthquake to destroy an enemy area.

We already have a good idea what causes an earthquake. They generally result from stresses in the earth's crust brought about by movement, or temperature changes deep below the ground causing tremendous strain upon the surface. Several scientists believe it should eventually prove fairly easy to trigger tremors by using a number of strategically placed explosions. It is known that an underground nuclear test often causes some rock movement.

Eyes down on a full world: an American spy plane on duty.

Eyes in the sky

Once upon a time only birds and stars were sighted in the skies. Nowadays they are joined by aeroplanes, rockets, spacemen and satellites whistling overhead. The world has become a very different place.

For one thing, everyone knows what everyone else is doing. The United States and Soviet Union alone have hundreds of satellites overhead, which act as large eyes in the sky. Although they circle as high as one mile (150 kilometres) above the earth, they are equipped with powerful cameras which can photograph even small objects like an automobile driving along a road, a small plane taking off, or a sailing boat skimming a lake.

Satellites can be manoeuvred. If countries suspect something is going on somewhere, they can 'hold' a satellite for long periods over whatever it is they want to watch. It is difficult to determine just how much these eyes can see. The governments which operate them keep the information secret.

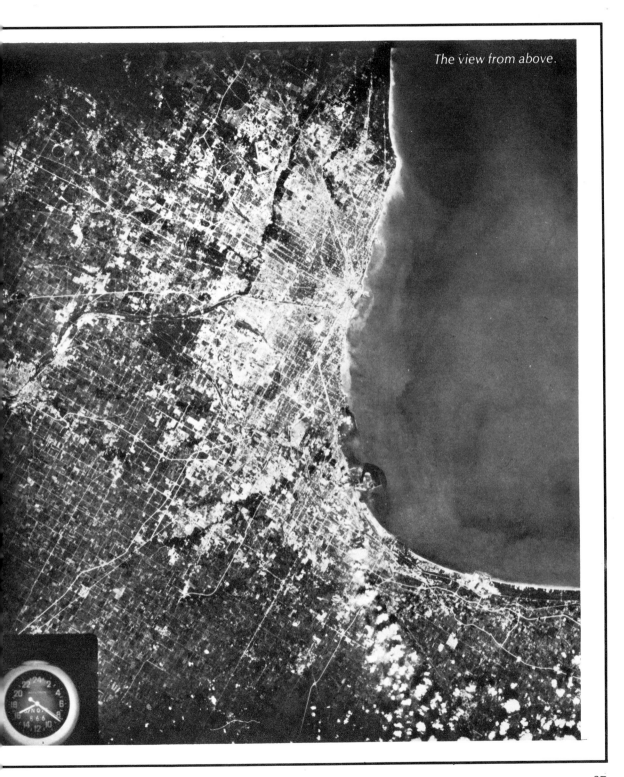

The view from above.

3 THE SWORD OF DAMOCLES

The first atomic bomb test, in July 1945 in America, melted the bomb's support tower. The American army put up a monument on the spot in 1965, which has come to be known as 'The Tomb of Humanity'.

'Every man, woman and child lives under a nuclear sword of Damocles, hanging by the slenderest of threads, capable of being cut at any moment by accident, miscalculation or madness. The weapons of war must be abolished before they abolish us.'

John F. Kennedy, addressing the UN General Assembly in 1961

The first bombs

It could happen.

A new conflict in the Middle East which finally engulfs the super powers, a serious incident along the East-West borders in Europe or a new 'Cuba' type crisis, could touch off a nuclear war so cataclysmic that life as we know it would come to a smouldering end. It is easy to say, 'It will never happen'. Yet accidents can and do happen, despite all precautions. The only way to stop an accident is to remove the risk.

Hiroshima in Japan gained itself a permanent place in history, on 6 August 1945, as the first city destroyed by a nuclear bomb. Three days later Nagasaki suffered the same terrible fate. Over 250,000 people are now known to have died as a result of the nuclear attack on Hiroshima, and about 60,000 in Nagasaki. The world will never know how many who survived the blasts are now dying of diseases caused so many years ago.

The lesson emerging from the horror bombings has not been learnt. Since that August day, when Hiroshima vanished in a flash of blinding light, the world has witnessed a build-up of an unbelievably high stockpile of nuclear weapons. The United States and the Soviet Union each now have enough nuclear weapons to blow themselves up many times over. In Europe alone there are about 7,000 American and 3,500 Soviet tactical nuclear weapons. Thousands more are scattered across the planet. The American stockpile of strategic and tactical nuclear weapons is the equivalent in explosive power of about 615,000 Hiroshima bombs. The Hiroshima blast killed over 250,000 people.

In 1945 there was only one nuclear power — the United States. Since then, the USSR, Britain, China, France and India have joined the nuclear club, and at least 20 other nations have the ability to develop and build a nuclear weapon.

Agreements on nuclear weapons have not always worked. In 1967, for example, the treaty of Tlatelolco was signed by many Latin American nations, in an effort to make the region a zone free of nuclear weapons. But Brazil and Argentina, the two countries with the ability to build and develop a nuclear weapon, have not fully accepted the treaty.

The nuclear dilemma started as little more than an interesting scientific venture earlier this century, when scientists realized it was possible to obtain energy by splitting the atom. The atom bomb is a very powerful explosive device, whose energy comes from the rapid 'fissioning' or breaking-up of many millions of atoms found in nuclear explosive materials such as uranium or plutonium. When an atom is split it releases neutrons, which travel outwards after being released. If they hit another atom they cause that to split too, and this in turn releases still more neutrons. If this process, known as a chain reaction, takes place extremely rapidly within an enclosed space, such as a bomb casing, the pressure becomes so great that an explosion takes place.

There are two techniques for triggering an atomic explosion. With the first method, two masses can be kept separate inside the bomb casing, but will explode as soon as they are brought together. The other method is known as implosion, and involves having the nuclear explosive material surrounded by a chemical explosive which, when it goes off, compresses the mass, forming a 'critical mass', leading to a sustained reaction, and finally a nuclear explosion.

August 6th 1945 Hiroshima

Hiroshima

JAPAN

Nagasaki

A hydrogen bomb, on the other hand, results from the rapid fusing of light atoms to form heavier ones. This results in a great release of explosive energy. In fact, the process occurs in much the same way as the sun produces light and heat. An H-bomb requires an atom bomb to trigger it.

At the start of World War II, scientists in many parts of the industrialised world knew it was possible to develop a nuclear bomb, but not how to develop it. Time, money and effort were needed. With the European nations fighting it out on the battlefield, it was perhaps natural that the conditions to develop the atom-bomb were found in the United States. Leading experts, like Professors Oppenheimer and Teller, were gathered in a small town in a New Mexico desert with a simple presidential order: Make a nuclear bomb! As the people of Hiroshima and Nagasaki discovered, the desert researchers succeeded. The bombs which destroyed these cities were crude. The explosive force of today's nuclear weapon is measured in either kilotons (Kt) — a thousand tons of TNT — or in megatons (mt), the equivalent of a million tons of TNT. Collectively, this form of measuring the explosive power is referred to as the 'yield'. Thus, the yield of the two bombs dropped on Hiroshima and Nagasaki were about 15 kilotons, equivalent to 15,000 tons of TNT.

The atom-bomb has a maximum yield of around 500 kilotons, or about 500,000 tons of TNT, while the H-bomb yield is almost unlimited. The Soviet Union, for example, tested during the mid-1960s a 57 metagon H-bomb, containing about 57 million tons of TNT, far more than the total tonnage of TNT used by either side during World War II.

The effects

When a nuclear weapon explodes it releases energy in the form of blast, heat and nuclear radiation. The degree of destruction caused by the explosion depends upon the height of the blast above the ground. Detonation first produces a gigantic fireball, then nuclear radiation, thermal (heat) radiation, ground shock, air blast and nuclear fallout. In the basic A-bomb, the incredibly rapid build-up of energy within a confined area caused by the splitting of hundreds of millions of atoms leads to an explosion with several tens of millions of degrees' temperature.

The fireball grows rapidly in size. Within seven-tenths of a milli-second — one-thousandth of a second — the fireball from a one megaton bomb is about 440 feet across and rising upwards at the rate of about 300 feet per second. After ten seconds the fireball is one and a quarter miles wide.

Its temperature drops rapidly as the fiery mass ascends and increases in size. A radio-active cloud forms. This cloud contains various debris and small drops of water from the air. The closer the explosion is to the ground, the more debris there is, as it causes strong updrafts of wind which suck dirt and other debris into the

radio-active cloud, contaminating it. Just 30 seconds after the explosion of a one megaton bomb, the cloud will have rocketed upwards to a height of about three and a half miles. It usually reaches its maximum height of 80,000 feet in about ten minutes.

Order me a transparent coffin and dig my crazy grave

After the next war … and the sky
Heaves with contaminated rain.
End to end our bodies lie
Round the world and back again.

Now from their concrete suites below
Statesmen demurely emanate,
And down the line of millions go
To see the people lie in state.

Nikita Ikes, Franco de Gaulles,
Officiate and dig the holes.
Mao tse-Sheks, Macadenauers,
Toting artificial flowers.

As they pay tribute each one wishes
The rain was less like tears, less hot, less thick.
They mutter, wise as blind white fishes,
Occasionally they are sick.

But I drily grin from my perspex coffin
As they trudge till they melt into the wet,
And I say: 'Keep on walking, keep on walking,
You bastards, you've got a hell of a way to walk yet.

Adrian Mitchell

As the cloud reaches its peak, the contaminated dirt and water start falling back towards the ground, causing widespread nuclear contamination. The seriousness of the fallout depends upon the height at which the nuclear device was exploded. If it exploded high above the ground, there would be less contamination; not as much debris would be sucked into the radio-active cloud. The Hiroshima and Nagasaki bombs, for example, were detonated about 1,800 and 1,500 feet up respectively above ground level, and as a result there was only limited fallout. However, a blast at surface level would result in very serious fallout, which would not only cause casualties but also make exposed food sources inedible and water undrinkable, and the affected area generally uninhabitable for a long time.

Much depends, of course, upon weather conditions at the time of the blast. Wind speed and direction play a big role in determining the extent of contamination and which areas will be affected. In 1954, the United States tested a 15 megaton thermonuclear device at Bikini atoll which seriously contaminated over 7,000 square miles. The fallout stretched roughly 20 miles upwind of the island and 320 miles downwind; the width was about 60 miles. The process of contamination took about ten hours. This test made it evident that cities like London, New York, Moscow, Paris and Tokyo could easily be made uninhabitable for a long time.

Much of the initial destruction results from the blast wave, which emanates at the explosion point. The tiniest fraction of a second after the explosion, a high-pressure wave builds up and moves away from the explosion. The front of the wave resembles a wall of compressed air, speeding along faster than the fastest express train. The shock wave from a one megaton bomb, for example, will have travelled almost four and a half miles within ten seconds of the explosion. After just one minute, the blast wave is twelve miles from the detonation point.

The blast wave from an ordinary non-nuclear bomb, fierce though it is, will usually only damage the part of a building closest to the detonation. The shock wave from a nuclear bomb, on the other hand, has much the same effect as an earthquake: it surrounds and destroys a building in much the same way as a tidal wave.

In Hiroshima and Nagasaki it was discovered that light buildings such as houses were very seriously damaged by blast, and then completely destroyed by fire. Large steel structures such as factories were stripped bare of roofing and walls by the blast wave, resulting in twisted, skeleton-like shells. Other buildings leaned like the Tower of Pisa, as though they had been struck by some stupendous wind.

If the blast wave does much of the intitial damage, heat or thermal radiation finishes the job. The fireball emits a first heat wave lasting only a fraction of a second. It is of extremely high temperature and includes a burst of ultra-violet radiation. The ultra-violet can cause serious eye damage, resulting in temporary or permanent blindness for those looking in the direction of the explosion when it occurs. The higher the blast in the air, the greater the risk of widespread retinal damage. A test carried out in the Pacific in 1958 gave a very good indication of the type of injuries that would be caused over a wide area. A 20 megaton bomb was exploded fifty miles above the surface of the earth. Rabbits over 345 miles away suffered retinal burns.

The United States Atomic Energy Commission believes that a major nuclear explosion sixty miles up could cause temporary or permanent loss of vision for any human who looked at the blast up to seven hundred miles away. A one-megaton bomb explosion would almost certainly destroy the sight of any human caught in the open up to three hundred miles away, and not necessarily looking directly at the blast.

This would all happen within about a tenth of a second. But then a second heat or thermal wave follows immediately on the heels of the first, and lasts about ten seconds. Although temperatures are generally much lower than in the first wave, the new heat wave causes skin burns for those exposed up to twelve miles from the burst of a one megaton bomb. The closer a person is to the explosion, the worse the burns.

After the bomb was over: Hiroshima, August 1945.

A burned body, Nagasaki, 1945.

Civilians being burnt alive in a nuclear attack. A moment from Peter Watkins' film The War Game.

Hiroshima and Nagasaki

The only real clues pointing to the extent and type of casualties which could result from a nuclear attack have come from the bombings of Hiroshima and Nagasaki. It has been estimated that 50 per cent of the deaths in the two Japanese bombings resulted from burns. Anyone within half a mile of the initial blast point was very lucky to have survived — and those who did ran a far greater risk of dying a few weeks later from radiation sickness than those further away from the explosion.

The human effect of the A-bomb. This Hiroshima victim had the fretwork of her dress burnt into her skin.

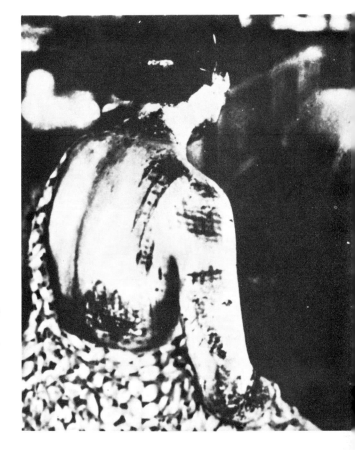

A person in an area subjected to a nuclear attack is likely to suffer either from direct or indirect burns. The heat from a nuclear blast (the experts call it thermal radiation) either burns the skin directly, as in sunburn cases, or indirectly from fire. Direct burns are called 'flash burns', as they are caused by the flash from the fireball, while indirect burns are known as 'flame burns'.

It has been estimated that a one megaton blast at ground level would cause widespread fires up to a distance of five miles from blast point, and a number of smaller fires up to seven miles away. Most of those treated for burns in the two bombed Japanese cities had suffered flash burns, and only about five per cent had flame burns. This was due to the fact that many of those who would have suffered flame burns died trapped in burning buildings. Most of the flame burns amongst survivors resulted from ignition of clothing due to the great heat; many had serious burns over much of their bodies.

Generally, a flash burn is only suffered on parts of the body exposed and facing in the direction of the explosion, mainly because most heat radiation travels in a straight line. A flash burn is usually not as dangerous as a flame burn, because the 'flash' resulting from an explosion lasts for only a fraction of a second — although the bigger the bomb, the bigger and more serious the burn. However, the Japan bombings revealed that those very close to the blast risk being burnt despite clothing, especially in areas where clothing was drawn tightly over the body, as in shoulder and elbow regions. Although the majority of those who suffered flash burns were outside, a surprisingly large number of people were burnt indoors. Many curtainless windows were open because it was a warm day.

Infection was a major problem in treating Japanese burn victims. In the devastation, with the lack of sanitation and adequate medical care, it was almost impossible to prevent it. It also would appear that nuclear radiation lessened bodily resistance to infection.

A phenomenon which appeared in Japan after the most serious burns had healed was the formation of thick overgrowths of scar tissue, known as keloids. It was first believed the keloids resulted from exposure to nuclear radiation, but further research has shown that they are due to abnormal growth of scar tissue in the burn wound, especially when healing is delayed by infection or malnutrition. Keloids were also found among badly burnt survivors from the American incendiary bomb raids on Tokyo during the war. However, the keloid scar generally diminishes in time.

I would be a witness for Hiroshima

I wish, as a survivor,
To be a real human being;
Besides, as a poor mother,
Fearing some day when the blue sky
Above the red-cheeked children
And those thousands with promising futures
Be smashed to atoms all of a sudden,
Endangering their bright futures
And now, to be repeated at a nation's cost,
I resolve to shed tears supposed to be shed on
   dead bodies,
Afresh for those people living now,
Declaring against all war, first of all.
Even if I should perchance be punished under a
   disgraceful name —
From a mother's protest against death for her
   own son's sake,
I should never dare to hide myself, never!
Because the day was too much impressed on my
   retina,
The hellish day of the fateful blaze.

It was August 6th in 1945,
At an early hour of the day;
Men and women were to start their daily work,
When unexpectedly the city and all were blown
   away,
Blistered hideously, each and all;
The seven rivers were filled with naked corpses.
Imagine a tale of the inferno,
Which he caught a glimpse of once,
And wants to tell of himself, when he is called
   the lord of the inferno,
I would go wherever it is, as a witness of the
   Hiroshima Tragedy,
That I might proclaim its misery;
I would sing for my life
'No more wars on the earth!'

Sadako Kurihara, a survivor of Hiroshima

How the H-bomb might destroy Tokyo, in three easy stages.

"Crikey! Have we got to start all over again?''

A cartoon from The Daily Mirror *days after the first bomb was dropped forecast the dangers of total destruction.*

Radiation

The most terrifying aspect of nuclear bombing is radiation. Early scare stories, suggesting that a nuclear blitzed area would prove uninhabitable for fifty years or more, have proved exaggerated. But life in a heavily bombed zone would probably not be the same for some time. Water and soil would have to be filtered many times to remove any radio-active materials; it would be impossible to permit cattle to eat grass and other roots exposed to radiation; while living accommodation would have to be either de-contaminated or rebuilt.

Exposure to radiation emanating from X-rays, gamma rays and neutrons, for example, can cause death. Nuclear radiation can attack the cells in living tissue, and in some cases destroy them. Radiation can also speed up the production of cells, causing cancer; it can affect parts of cells, causing genetic defects; or it can halt production of new cells to replace those dying off naturally.

The effect of nuclear radiation on the body varies, of course, depending upon the total dosage and, to some extent, upon the period of time during which it is absorbed. The parts most sensitive to nuclear radiation are the lymphoid tissues, bone marrow, spleen, reproduction organs and gastro-intestinal tract. Skin, lungs and liver are the next most sensitive areas, while muscle, nerves and adult bones are the least vulnerable. Children's bones and organs, especially, are very sensitive to radiation.

Survivors of a nuclear attack would probably start to show the first signs of radiation sickness within two hours. It begins with nausea and vomiting. A few hours later the survivor becomes listless, has no desire to eat and feels tired most of the time. Production of vital white blood cells, which fight infection, is inhibited, and declines. This means that wounds will either take much longer to heal, or will not heal at all. After about two weeks, the victim's hair starts to fall out.

Chances of survival depend upon the degree of exposure. Those exposed to a very large amount of radiation experience internal bleeding about two to three weeks after the attack. Blood may be found in urine, for example, due to bleeding in the kidney. Because of the slowdown of white blood cell production, infection sets in, and sores break out around the lips before spreading throughout the mouth and the gastro-intestinal tract. Death can occur anytime between the second and eighth week after exposure to nuclear radiation.

In Japan it was found that patients who managed to hang on to life for three to four months had a fairly good recovery rate. Hair began to regrow and white cells started reproducing. A survivor of a nuclear raid who has been exposed to a high level of nuclear radiation does have a slim chance of survival if the right treatment is readily available.

Long term radiation effects are more frightening. Leukemia, genetic defects, retarded development, malignant diseases and a shortened life span are some of the possibilities. Survivors of Hiroshima and Nagasaki saw an increase of leukemia. Pregnant women exposed to nuclear radiation had a higher rate of still births as well as deaths of infant children. Five years after the bombs were dropped, a study of children who had survived the blasts showed a slightly increased frequency of mental retardation. In 1952, a comparison of children exposed to nuclear radiation with

They killed him before he was born

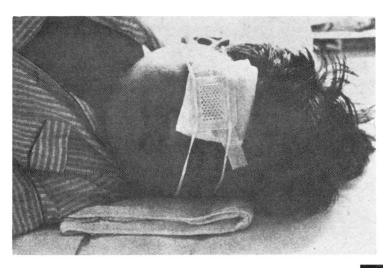

This boy was killed by an atom bomb dropped before he was born. The father was exposed to radiation of the Hiroshima atom bomb as a young student; but he survived and after some years married. A child was born — and it developed radiation sickness. This picture was taken a month before it died when already it showed the purple spots that are a sign of approaching death and when its eye was bandaged to stop cerebral haemorrhage.

normal children the same age showed a somewhat lower average body weight, stature and maturity.

In March 1954 a nuclear test in the Pacific went awry when the Americans underestimated the power of the explosion and a group of islanders on the Marshall Islands were exposed to fallout. The catastrophe provided grisly information for researchers.

Fallout dropped on the islands about five hours after the explosion, and resembled large fluffy flakes of snow. The islanders had no idea what the mysterious flakes could be, and as a result simply went about their business after their initial curiosity had worn off. But soon many of them noticed an itchy feeling on parts of the

body exposed and touched by the powder — mostly the head, bare shoulders and feet. Some experienced a mild burning sensation. Two or three weeks later skin sores resembling burns and lesions erupted on parts of the body infected with fallout. Although most of the lesions were only superficial, there were more serious cases in which the sores ulcerated and oozed. Hair fell out in many cases. No immediate long-term effects were noted, however, and with regular treatment the great majority of islanders were reported fully healed in six months, with hair growing back again. But it was later discovered that about 80 per cent of the children on the island had damaged thyroid glands, and would experience trouble in later years.

From the mid-1950s to the early 1960s, there was a rash of books and articles describing how the world could come to an end because of long-term radiation resulting from a large nuclear war. It is doubtful if this could happen overnight, or even over a few weeks, but tests with animals have shown that nuclear radiation does lead to an increased frequency of gene mutations. This belief that the planet could finally be populated by mutated humans is not as far fetched as some government leaders want us to believe. In fact, it is now common to use radiation to 'doctor' a seed to produce a different type of flower or vegetable.

Long-term fallout is carried hundreds of thousands of miles by the wind stream, and is deposited into the soil by rain or snow. It soon gets into the food chain. A contaminated plant is eaten by an animal, the animal is eaten by man, who dies and returns to the soil. Thus works the terrible circuit of contamination.

Of all the radio-active substances injected into our environment by a nuclear explosion, only a few are considered to be really harmful so far as internal contamination is concerned. Strontium 90 and Celsium 137, in particular, are deadly in the long run. Both cause bone tumours and anaemia, leukemia and necrosis (the death of some part of the body). Widespread public fears about fallout led to the Soviet Union, the United States and Britain agreeing in 1963 to ban the testing of nuclear weapons in the atmosphere. But the number of possible deaths and tragedies which resulted from nuclear testing will never be known.

'Don't hit me, or . . .'

Since 1945 the two super-powers have leaned on the 'deterrent' theory as the most effective way to maintain peace. Deterrence means convincing a potential enemy that it would not prove worthwhile to instigate a nuclear attack; the retaliatory damage would outweigh whatever would be gained. It is rather like walking along a tightrope, meeting someone moving in the opposite direction and telling him that if he pushes you off, you'll make sure he tumbles with you. Deadlock remains until some agreement is reached whereby you can get past one another, or until one side gets tired, slips or makes an accidental move, which is misinterpreted by the other side as an act of aggression — ending in mutual destruction.

Over the past few years, the major powers have devised an evasive new vocabulary to describe current strategic thinking. A 'first-strike capability', for example, is an initial attack aimed at destroying another nation's ability to retaliate, while the ability to retaliate during or after an attack is known as a 'second-strike capability'. First-strike capability can only be regarded as successful if an enemy is completely wiped out.

Perhaps the most worrying development was the decision by the United States to underline the importance of 'counter-force' strategy, which may be interpreted as a step towards a 'first-strike capability'. Counter-force calls for development of more accurate, but less powerful nuclear weapons to permit the military to conduct 'surgical strikes'. It is argued that small nuclear weapons, used on the battlefield, would reduce the risk of civilian losses. It's a type of reasoning which amounts to a short cut to suicide. Aside from the radiation risks, the main danger stems from the notion that even one nuclear weapon can be deployed without triggering escalation.

It became clear during the late 1950s that it was more than feasible to develop a 'mini-nuke' for battlefield use. As early as 1953, the US army devised an artillery gun that could fire a nuclear shell with a 15 kiloton yield — about the same size bomb which destroyed Hiroshima. Mini-nuclear weapons, it is argued, provide a 'limited' alternative to global nuclear war. This type of reasoning naturally depends upon the sanity of the leaders of the countries involved, and their ability not to lose their tempers or panic should the tide turn against them on the battlefield.

The effectiveness of the mini-nuclear warhead on the battlefield can also be questioned. On the odd few occasions that the United States and their European allies held military exercises in which limited nuclear weapons were theoretically used, total confusion prevailed. In one exercise in the mid-1950s, it was determined that 1.7 million people would have died and three million been wounded. The lesson learnt was that the use of mini-nukes on the battlefield would have to be strictly controlled.

Attempts have of course been made by world leaders to argue that nuclear weapons of all types are necessary, that nuclear warfare in the future could be a relatively 'clean' and 'limited' affair. Over the past three decades there has been a massive build-up of nuclear weapons, principally by the two super-powers. At the end of World War II the number of nuclear weapons in existence could have been counted on one hand. Today, they exist in tens of thousands. In 1972, the year the strategic arms limitation agreement was signed, the United States alone had 1,054 intercontinental ballistic missiles (ICBMs), while the Soviet Union had 1,527.

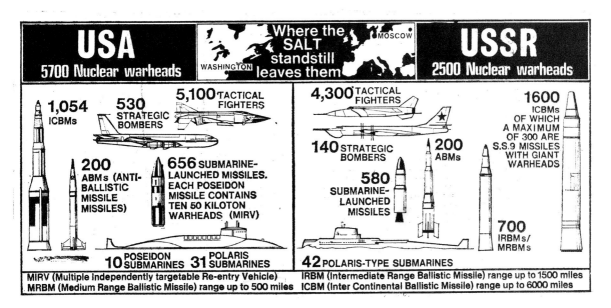

USA
5700 Nuclear warheads

Where the SALT standstill leaves them

MOSCOW
WASHINGTON

USSR
2500 Nuclear warheads

1,054 ICBMs
530 STRATEGIC BOMBERS
5,100 TACTICAL FIGHTERS
200 ABMs (ANTI-BALLISTIC MISSILE MISSILES)
656 SUBMARINE-LAUNCHED MISSILES. EACH POSEIDON MISSILE CONTAINS TEN 50 KILOTON WARHEADS (MIRV)
10 POSEIDON SUBMARINES
31 POLARIS SUBMARINES

4,300 TACTICAL FIGHTERS
140 STRATEGIC BOMBERS
200 ABMs
580 SUBMARINE-LAUNCHED MISSILES
1600 ICBMs OF WHICH A MAXIMUM OF 300 ARE S.S.9 MISSILES WITH GIANT WARHEADS
700 IRBMs/MRBMs
42 POLARIS-TYPE SUBMARINES

MIRV (Multiple Independently targetable Re-entry Vehicle)
MRBM (Medium Range Ballistic Missile) range up to 500 miles

IRBM (Intermediate Range Ballistic Missile) range up to 1500 miles
ICBM (Inter Continental Ballistic Missile) range up to 6000 miles

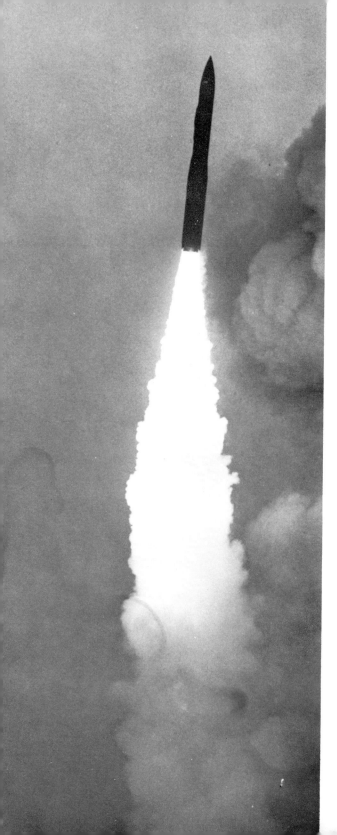

Missile launch.

Getting on target

While the missile build-up has continued, nuclear weapon technology has not only kept apace, but accelerated. Guidance and accuracy have been greatly improved. This in turn means increased tension between the super-powers. Although the bomber is still considered a delivery vehicle for a nuclear weapon, the mainstay of a modern strategic nuclear strike force is the ballistic missile. Those that can travel up to 1,500 miles (2,400 kms) are known as Medium Range Ballistic Missiles (MRBM). Those that have a range between 1,500 miles, (2,400 kms) and 4,000 miles (6,400 kms) are called Intermediate Range Ballistic Missiles (IRBM), while those capable of travelling over 4,000 miles (6,400 kms) are known as Intercontinental Ballistic Missiles (ICBM).

The real terror weapon is the missile-packing nuclear submarine. Missiles launched from under the water by submarines — known as Submarine Launched Ballistic Missiles (SLBM) — are the weapons currently causing the most concern to general staffs and peace researchers alike. On the move all the time, and prowling in the depths of the world's oceans, the strategic nuclear submarine is almost invulnerable to attack. Yet each submarine packs enough nuclear missiles to destroy vast areas of enemy territory. Both the Americans and the Soviets are now building up their strategic nuclear submarine fleets as quickly as possible.

Nowadays a modern long-range strategic missile has a good chance of landing within a half-mile radius of its target. In a few years a bull's-eye hit will be a near certainty, because missile silos are now being 'superhardened', or reinforced, to withstand anything except a direct hit.

'It started with one of their pigeons pecking one of ours.'

To improve the chances of a 'bull's-eye' hit, multiple warheads for strategic missiles are being developed. The first multiple warhead missile was the MRV, or multiple re-entry vehicle. This consists of several warheads being dispersed over the target area in shotgun fashion, so that they fall in a close pattern on and around it, increasing the chances of scoring a direct hit.

The next step was MIRV, a multiple, independently targetable re-entry vehicle, which uses a more sophisticated system to direct individual warheads towards widely separated targets. As many as 14 MIRVs can be fitted onto the American 'Poseidon' SLBM, for example. The MIRV is now being superseded by the MARV — Manoeuvrable Re-entry Vehicle — a warhead with a guidance system that allows it to correct course during the final part of the flight path, and thus home in on the target with pinpoint accuracy.

These technical advances, especially the MARV, increase the chance of either the US or the Soviet Union being able to wipe out their opponent's entire land-based missile force. This 'first-strike capability' increases the risk of attack in the event of a major world political crisis. It is a development that makes the nuclear balance of terror more precarious and unstable.

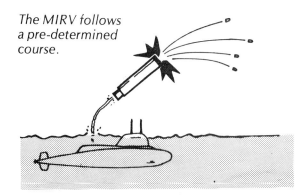

The MIRV follows a pre-determined course.

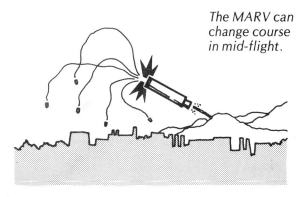

The MARV can change course in mid-flight.

Showing off to the world: some Russian rockets are paraded through Moscow.

Where will it all end?

In the meantime, as the atomic arms race goes on, the public continues to be brainwashed into believing that either a nuclear war cannot happen, or that if it does, it will not be as bad as everyone fears. But the only possible end of course would be catastrophe. The super-powers have a vast arsenal of tactical nuclear weapons designed for 'limited' purposes. But what is meant by 'limited'? It has been estimated that the total explosive power of existing tactical nuclear weapons is roughly equivalent to 50,000 Hiroshima type bombs.

There are those who argue that the existence of nuclear weapons has stopped the eruption of a major war between the super-powers. These theorists stand on extremely shaky ground. The only evidence they can produce is that a

nuclear war has not happened. They also argue that the existence of nuclear weapons has reduced the risk of conventional warfare — conveniently ignoring the wars in the Middle East, Africa and Indochina. Millions of people have died and millions more have undergone untold suffering in conventional conflicts since 1945.

Mr. Robert McNamara, while he was U.S. Secretary of Defence, made a classic 'deterrent' statement in 1967, which summoned up American and probably Soviet military thinking: 'We must be able to absorb the total weight of nuclear attack on our country — on our strike-back forces, on our cities, and on our population — and still be fully capable of destroying the aggressor.' Bearing in mind the current nuclear weapons arsenals of the United

'All God's chillun got N-power.

States and the Soviet Union, it is not difficult to foresee the result of all-out nuclear warfare between the two. The very existence of these weapons of mass destruction in such huge quantities itself poses a threat to world security.

The construction of huge warships as a 'deterrent' by each of the major powers prior to 1914 did not stop World War I, and the threat of 'total war' did not avert World War II. How, then, is a nuclear war halted if one side seriously believes it can wipe out most of the enemy's retaliatory weapons before they even leave the ground — only to discover minutes later that such a presumption was deadly wrong? There are no winners in nuclear war.

Dr. Bernard T. Feld, professor of physics at the Massachusetts Institute of Technology, and an expert on the history of disarmament negotiations, predicted in 1975 that 'the odds are around one in three that a nuclear weapon will be used in a conflict situation before the

year 1984, and the chances are even worse for nuclear war to occur in the years remaining in this century.' A nuclear war, or even a so-called 'limited' nuclear conflict, would spell the end of life as we know it. A single megaton bomb striking the centre of a large city would create a crater over 300 feet (100 metres) deep and over 1.8 miles (three kilometres) in diameter. The fireball resulting from the blast would extend over 2.6 miles (four kilometres) and temperatures within the blast area would be in the region of 4,500 degrees centigrade. Widespread devastation and hundreds of thousands of casualties would occur for miles around the impact area, and radiation would create long-term genetic defects and cancers in humans, animals and plant life.

Despite all of the 'arms control' agreements, the nuclear race continues. Time is running out. The consequences of nuclear war demand an immediate re-awakening of public interest, and protests on a global scale.

The vocabulary of death

MRV (Multiple Re-entry Vehicle) Missile with several warheads to fall in a close pattern around the target.

MIRV (Multiple Independently targetable Re-entry Vehicle) Missile with a number of warheads targeted for independent objectives.

MARV (Manoeuvrable Re-entry Vehicle) Missile with several warheads which can be independently manoeuvred as they near their separate targets.

Strategic nuclear weapons Long-range weapons carried on either ICBMs or SLBMs or long-range bombers.

Tactical nuclear weapons Short-range weapons carried on smaller missiles.

Mini-nukes A very small nuclear weapon for battlefield use, or for severing an opponent's lines of communication.

ICBM (Intercontinental Ballistic Missile) Range about 4,000 miles.

IRBM (Intermediate-Range Ballistic Missile) Range between 1,500 and 4,000 miles.

MRBM (Medium-Range Ballistic Missile) Range about 1,500 miles.

SLBM (Submarine-Launched Ballistic Missile) Main advantage stems from submarine's invisibility. No one can be sure where a strike might come from a range of 2,500 miles or more.

ABM (Anti-Ballistic Missile) A missile packing a nuclear warhead, aimed at incoming attack missiles. Owing to the high degree of technical sophistication needed, both the US and Soviet Union have generally rejected them.

ASW (Anti-Submarine Warfare) Aimed at detecting and destroying submarines, which are hard to detect.

MAD (Mutual Assured Destruction) When each side has convinced the other of its ability to wipe it out, a MAD situation has been reached.

Overkill To be able to kill or destroy an opponent more than once. At the moment the US and Soviet Union can wipe each other out about ten times.

'You can overkill us 50 times, but we can only overkill you 49 times.'

60

The day the *Lucky Dragon's* luck ran out

At about five o'clock on the morning of 1 March 1954, the sky over Bikini Atoll in the Pacific was lit by a flash brighter than the noonday sun. The United States had just exploded a powerful hydrogen bomb.

About 80 miles (140 kilometres) away, a tiny Japanese fishing boat was drifting slowly along, a net lowered over the side. As the bomb flash lit the sky, one of the crew remarked: 'The sun rises in the west today.' A few minutes later the boat rocked as the blast wave from the explosion swept past, and about ninety minutes later an ash-like substance fell from the sky, coating the boat and twenty-three crew members as if it were snow.

Luckily, perhaps, the trawler had concluded its fishing trip. But during the two-week voyage back to port the crew began suffering a variety of ailments. Some had burn-like wounds on their bodies, while others felt run-down and generally 'sick.' Not until they returned to port did the crew discover that it had been exposed to radiation fallout. They were dispatched to hospital in Tokyo, where one later died.

The trawler, *Fukuryu Maru* (*Lucky Dragon*), and its catch were immediately isolated. The fish were found to have been heavily contaminated, and were burnt, while the boat was decontaminated several times before being abandoned on a rubbish dump known as the Island of Dreams. The boat has since been restored, to serve as another reminder of the horror of nuclear weapons.

4 ALL THE KING'S HORSES...

The biggest sleeping airforce in the world, Tucson, Arizona. Six thousand obsolete bombers and fighters worth $6 billion.

'The world now stands at the most critical crossroads. It can pursue the arms race at a terrible price to the security and progress of the peoples of the world, or it can move ahead towards the goal of general and complete disarmament.'

U Thant, Secretary General of the United Nations, 1969.

Selling power

Arms merchants, both private and government, are interested in profits, and not 'right' or 'wrong' causes. An embargo on sales to a particular nation or region is often an open invitation for them. When Britain in 1964 refused to sell weapons to South Africa, France stepped in. During the 1950s and early 1960s the United States placed restrictions on sales of advanced weaponry to Latin America. But towards the end of the decade many European arms producers moved into the vacuum.

Merchants of death are nothing if not versatile. One private American arms dealer boasts that he can fully equip a small army and keep it supplied in the field with spare parts.

At the end of World War II only five countries — the United States, the Soviet Union, Britain, Canada and Sweden — had the facilities and know-how to produce advanced weapons. Nowadays over thirty countries mass produce 'sophisticated' weaponry, whose characteristics for killing, maiming and destroying are candidly described in sales catalogues.

Today the four major weapons producers are the United States, the Soviet Union, France and Britain. But many other countries have fingers in the pie. Even non-aligned Sweden, which officially bans sales of weapons to 'tension areas', has no trouble exporting death-dealing products. West Germany, prevented from producing weapons until the mid-1950s, quietly maintains a large arms industry, exporting warships, tanks and mines as well as other items. There are strong pressures within the Federal Republic to 'bolster' the economy by going into the arms business in a big way.

According to the Stockholm International Peace Research Institute (SIPRI), an estimated 600,000 highly qualified scientists and engineers throughout the world are employed full-time on military research and development. They are bent on 'improving' and perfecting existing weaponry and designing and developing tomorrow's arsenals. In 1976 world military expenditure was $250 thousand million: for several years the world has spent more on armaments than on education, and twice as much than on public health. In underdeveloped countries, where improved health and education are urgently needed, the ratio favouring arms expenditure is even higher.

Hello to arms

Arms industries, together with the arms race, came into being during the latter half of the nineteenth century, when metallurgical and engineering advances were seized upon by general staffs. At the same time faster communication links provided by the railroad and mechanized vehicles meant it was easier to mobilise large armies and transport them across great distances quickly. Science thus loomed increasingly in military thinking.

Vast armaments concerns emerged, like Krupp in Germany and Vickers in Britain. Sir Basil Zaharoff, chief salesman of Vickers, made a fortune by selling arms to both sides during the Boer War and World War I. And as munition companies grew in wealth and industrial clout, they were able to wield enormous political power, which many used to full advantage. A League of Nations report in 1921 tartly noted that 'wars are promoted by the competitive zeal of private armament firms.'

The German arms industry in the 1920s, drawn by George Grosz.

Sir Edward Grey, British Foreign Secretary, declared on the eve of World War I that 'the moral is obvious: it is that great armaments lead inevitably to war. If there are armaments on one side, there must be armaments on the other side.... Each measure taken by one nation is noted and leads to counter-measures by others.'

He added that the increase in armaments which is 'intended in each nation to produce consciousness of strength, and a sense of security, does not produce these effects. On the contrary, it produces a consciousness of the strength of other nations and a sense of fear. Fear begets suspicion and distrust and evil imaginings of all sorts, till each government feels it would be criminal and a betrayal of its own country not to take every precaution of every other government as evidence of hostile intent....'

Sir Edward's observation can be borne in mind when contemplating the contemporary scene. As big-power delegates sit at conference tables discussing arms limitations, other representatives of their countries — latter-day Zaharoffs — scurry about hawking the wares of torture and mass violence.

Biggest spenders on military hardware are the two super-powers. The United States and the Soviet Union together account for two-thirds of total world military expenditure. Many believe the basic reason for the arms race since 1945 has been a struggle for political or economic supremacy between Washington and Moscow. In the immediate post-war years this was certainly true, but the theory no longer holds water. Otherwise, the gradual improvement of relations between East and West would have seen a slackening of the arms race, with fear and mistrust replaced by sanity.

Research and development

A basic reason for the current arms race is 'runaway' technology — the compulsive desire to keep apace with new weapons 'the other side' might be developing. Military research and development now gobble up a sizeable chunk of the military budget. The two super-powers together spend more on research than total defence spending in any other country, with the possible exception of China.

Since World War II there has been a trebling in world military spending. A SIPRI study noted that this massive jump in expenditure is not the result of large armies or greater quantities of weapons, but is incurred because of the nebulous need to 'update' arsenals. Each successive generation of weapons cost more to research, develop and manufacture, as well as to operate and maintain. It can take ten years for a new plane to move from drawing board to mass production. Before its first test flight another generation is being planned.

To make matters worse, the super-powers are convinced that in addition to 'keeping up' in research and development they must also try to forecast possible future developments in enemy weaponry. Weapons researchers, operating on the theory that nothing is impossible, are thus given a more-or-less free hand to set into motion programmes aimed at protecting their country against as many possible developments as they can conceive. This, in turn, calls for new and expensive technologies, and as the weapons become even more complex, the technical and industrial capacity created by them becomes greater. The snowball gets bigger and bigger, diverting more and more money and resources from worthwhile endeavours, such as stamping out famine and poverty.

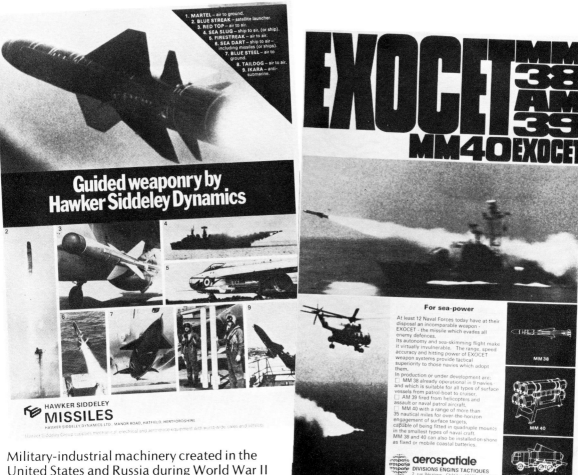

Military-industrial machinery created in the United States and Russia during World War II and the Korean War has never been cut back. Powerful bureaucratic and economic forces within these countries have successfully beaten back all efforts to cut their size. During the 'Cold War' years these forces had a heyday. Tension and fear in Europe was high, and military establishments, backed by arms industries, cashed in. They were not slow in pointing out that military power not only 'deterred' possible attacks, but could also contribute to a country's bargaining power at negotiating tables. In addition, politicians are generally loathe to stop construction of a munitions plant or development of new weapons systems, as it affects jobs in their districts. Little thought is given to the possibility of starting more worthwhile industries.

The arms race between the super-powers has made it essential for smaller arms-producing nations to export their products, in order to keep up with spiralling research and development costs. Although exporting countries such as France and Britain, West Germany, Italy and Sweden have the know-how to produce a wide range of sophisticated weapons, their home markets are too small to cover costs.

Emphasis upon development and exploitation of technology for military purposes has meant an enormous increase in the cost of weapons systems and related equipment. There are also hidden costs, such as the ever-growing demand for skilled personnel to operate and maintain new equipment. Not only are there more military personnel than ever before — a 20 per cent rise since 1955 — but their education and training costs have spiralled.

All the fun of the arms fair. Above: pretty rockets all in a row. Right: business seems quiet.

Some small arms change sides in Angola.

Dealing with weapons

The United States is still the dominant arms producer and, generally speaking, the most technologically advanced. The Soviet arms industry, while comprehensive, tends to concentrate upon basic designs which can easily be adapted for different roles — or improved with the passage of time. France and Britain lie third and fourth respectively, while weapons industries everywhere else tend to be comparatively small, and limited to less technically complicated products, such as light aircraft. In a number of countries, including China, West Germany, India and Israel, a major long-term expansion of weapon development and production has started.

Not much attention has been paid to the arms race in conventional weaponry, whose introduction into conflicts since World War I has caused the death of tens of millions. In fact, more money is allocated on a global basis to development and production of conventional weapons than to nuclear programmes. From 1964 to 1974 the international trade in non-nuclear arms increased by around 55 per cent, and annual turnover is about $9,000 million.

A recent development is the readiness of nations to sell even their most advanced weaponry. The United States, for example, has exported to several Middle East countries TOW, one of the world's most advanced remote-controlled anti-tank missiles. The Americans have also supplied Iran with F-14A jets, while the Russians have supplied Syria with Mig-23 warplanes. These two planes are among the most sophisticated aircraft now being manufactured, and they were made available for export within two years after entering production for domestic use.

The worldwide trade in weapons leads to strange situations. On occasion, opposing armies have met on battlefields with the same weapons and equipment supplied by the same source. Turks and Greeks packed American weapons when they clashed on the Mediterranean island of Cyprus in 1974, and American weapons were also used by both sides during the 1965 Indo-Pakistan War.

Arms dealers have recently latched onto a new gimmick. An American private defence contractor, with the tacit support of the Pentagon, is providing a Persian Gulf country with special military 'advisers.' These freelance mercenaries are required to have had combat experience, and their job is to teach the locals what modern non-nuclear war is about. Many Third World countries have recognized that it takes more than a well-equipped army to fight successfully, and this new service is high on the shopping list.

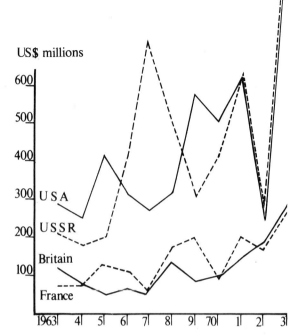

US$ millions

600	
500	
400	
300	USA
200	USSR
100	Britain
	France

1963 4 5 6 7 8 9 70 1 2 3

Arms sales to the third world.

Although military expenditure in the Third World is only a small fraction of the total, it is increasing every year. These countries are buying far more sophisticated weapons. In 1958 only four Third World countries had supersonic aircraft; by 1968 there were 28; and in 1974 the figure had climbed to 39. Instead of devoting limited economic resources to more essential needs, many developing countries are paying around 10 million dollars for each new jet plane.

The super-powers have provided many underdeveloped regions with every conceivable armament in a bid to gain influence. Conflicts which racked Southeast Asia, the Middle East and Africa lined the pockets of munition makers. The Third World scramble started when many countries achieved independence from former colonial powers, opening new markets for arms dealers. As each new nation purchased a glistening warplane or tank, others felt bound to follow suit, resulting in growing tension. France and Britain abetted these trends by opening the doors of their military academies to young officers from former colonial territories. It was a relatively easy way to retain some influence, and a very cheap way to promote sales of military equipment.

The arms sales race to the Third World picked up steam in the early 1950s, after a treaty between the United States, France and Britain limiting flow of weapons to the Middle East broke down. Since then, the super-powers have used arms sales to the Third World not only for political and economic gain, but also as a way to gain a foreign military outpost. In some cases, weapons sales have been made conditional upon provision of territory for bases: the facilities provided for the Soviet Union in the Yemen, and for the United States in Spain, are just two examples.

Loss of old markets is not fatal. When the Vietnam War ended, the Americans found new outlets in Latin America and the Middle East, which has seen fairly constant fighting since World War II. Now, thanks to oil revenues, many Middle East countries have money to burn. The Persian Gulf is one of the most heavily militarized zones in the world. There is a serious risk that the massive arms buildup will result in conflicts between Persian Gulf countries, who have no love for one another despite religious and cultural links. Their arsenals are equipped with missiles, tanks, jet planes and destroyers purchased from the United States, while other Gulf nations have bought heavy artillery, missiles and jets from the Soviet Union and France. Britain has weighed in with tanks.

'Explain slowly — what does he need all those weapons for, and why does he need nuclear reactors?'

Iran, for instance, now has one of the most modern and advanced arsenals in the world. Its air force is equipped with hundreds of American jets, such as the Gumman F14, which flies at twice the speed of sound. The Shah of Iran can also field 1,000 helicopters and 3,000 armoured vehicles. The Iranian navy includes a large number of destroyers, frigates and British-supplied military Hovercraft which can be equipped with missiles. The Iranian arms buildup not only worries other Persian Gulf nations, but also India. It fears a possible pact between Iran and Pakistan, and is wary of growing Iranian naval influence in the already tense Indian Ocean region.

Latin America has finally become enmeshed in the nets cast by arms dealers. In 1973 European nations were reported to have sold some $2,000 million of advanced weaponry to the region. Since then there has been a marked increase in tension and a revival of old border disputes.

Nuclear weapons are not yet being hawked by anyone. But it is probably only a question of time before another crisis, similar to the 1974 oil shortage, 'forces' a country to consider selling its nuclear know-how. Several industrialised nations are already supplying developing countries with technology for construction of nuclear-power plants.

Obviously, Third World countries are the first to gain from a rapid diminishment or halt to the worldwide arms trade. Yet they believe that failure to arm would leave them at the mercy of industrialised countries, who themselves generally avoid direct involvement in conflicts. The United States and Russia, who lead the industrialised pack, have cashed in on

deprivation and poverty for their political and economic benefit. 'The world is still dominated by too many rulers and groups who do not suit their actions to their words', said M. Réné Maheu, director-general of the United Nations Educational, Scientific and Cultural Organisation (UNESCO). They preach peace while waging or preparing for war, he said, exact justice while tolerating discrimination and flagrant inequality, 'pay lip service to progress while diverting to armaments enormous sums which they could more usefully spend on peaceful development both in their own countries and abroad'.

The arms race itself is the greatest single peril now facing the world, the United Nations said in a 1971 report. The race is far more dangerous than poverty or disease, far more dangerous than the population explosion or pollution. The world organisation said the threat of ultimate disaster created by the arms race 'far outweighs whatever short-term advantages armaments may have achieved in providing peoples with a sense of national security'.

Showing the flag — and a few other things beside

Red Square, Moscow

Cairo, Egypt

ВЬЕТНАМ ПОБЕДИТ !

АГРЕССОРА ВОН ИЗ ВЬЕТНАМА !

Kampala, Uganda

5 PEACE FOR OUR TIME?

Signing for world peace, China.

'Far from considering general and complete disarmament, the major powers are engaged in the greatest armaments race that has ever existed in the world. Negotiations are only aimed at limiting the increase of defensive weapons and the increase of ballistic nuclear weapons . . . The present negotiations do not relate to disarmament — they relate to phased armament.'

Sean MacBride, Nobel Peace Prize Winner, 1974

Signing for world peace, United States. Kennedy signs the Partial Nuclear Test Ban Treaty, Nixon the Nonproliferation Treaty, Ford the Peaceful Nuclear Explosion Treaty. Was it worth all that ink?

75

Attempts at control

There is no single path to the ideal of a disarmed world; history is littered with examples of arms-control measures. Over three thousand years ago the Philistines forced a defeated Israel to limit production of iron-tipped spears. In 201 BC Rome and Carthage, then in a bitter struggle for supremacy, outlawed the use of war elephants. Owing to their tendency to panic and run amok, these beasts were often more dangerous to the user than to the enemy.

The Catholic church tried to ban the use of the crossbow in wars between Christians, as the new weapon was considered to be too inhumane — except for use against non-Christians. During the nineteenth century, the United States and Britain reached agreement on prohibiting warships on the Great Lakes separating Canada and America. In more recent times, agreement was reached banning the use of poisonous gases, while the 1963 Test Ban treaty prohibited the explosion of nuclear devices in the atmosphere or above the ground. A 1967 treaty banned the orbiting of nuclear weapons above the earth.

However, most past efforts towards disarmament should be seen as attempts to control weaponry on a localized scale rather than moves towards banning all weapons of war. A common motivation for 'arms control' has been to assure that a vanquished foe is not given the chance to fight within the foreseeable future. Arms limitations were placed on Germany at the end of World Wars I and II, for instance, in an effort to end 'German militarism.'

Of course, there are other reasons why nations have gathered around negotiating tables to discuss 'control' or limitation. A country wedged between two opposing power blocs may consider it advisable, as Austria did in 1955, to sign agreements with the blocs to 'limit' its own weapons to purely defensive types, thus making its position as a neutral quite clear. Alternatively, a government may feel it politically desirable to divert funds from armaments to areas such as education or social welfare.

One might think that the obvious reason for nations to seriously discuss disarmament is to rid the world of the risk of total war. But decision-makers usually decide to discuss arms limitation because of rising costs. Some researchers feel that naval limitation pacts during the 1920s and 1930s resulted from a desire to divert money away from a naval arms race in order to cope with economic strains the industrialised world was then experiencing. Now, with raw material prices increasing fast, industrialised nations are faced with the same problem. Today's politicians must decide what comes first — a new warplane or a new school, a nuclear submarine or slum clearance, the latest German tank or a free milk scheme for school children.

Arguments 'for' and 'against' disarmament have not changed much in recent years. Those against disarmament argue that national security would be endangered, and that it would be impossible to determine whether another nation stuck to the bargain. They maintain that economic repercussions resulting from disarmament would lead to economic and social disorder, and that global disarmament is 'utopian' anyway, because it fails to take into account human aggression. They also point to the failure of earlier arms-control agreements or disarmament talks.

British munitions factory during World War I: how easy is it to find alternative jobs when the fighting is done?

According to those who favour disarmament, it has been clearly demonstrated that when the will is there, it is possible to reach agreement on controlling or eliminating weaponry. Substantial reductions in armaments industry employment have also been accomplished successfully in the past without disruption of national economies.

Between August 1945 and June 1946, the size of the United States armed forces was reduced by over nine million men. Despite the rapid cutback, careful planning ensured that the 1946 unemployment rate stayed below 4 per cent. In Britain, some nine million people, or 42 per cent of the working population, were involved in the armaments industries in 1945. The figure had been slashed to two million 16 months later. Over five million people found civilian jobs, 700,000 were unemployed, while the other 1.2 million voluntarily stopped working. At no time did unemployment rise above 4 per cent. Nowadays, if Britain decided to disarm immediately, less than two million persons would require alternative occupations.

Some 50 million people in the world are either directly or indirectly involved in military-directed occupations, either in the armed forces or industrial activities geared towards armaments. How many vital raw materials now in short supply are being devoted to military purposes will probably never be known.

Perhaps the biggest stumbling block to disarmament is the deterrent theory, now under severe criticism. Nations with high armament levels or regions heavily militarized tend to be involved in war more than countries with relatively low armaments levels.

Those who favour the 'deterrent' theory often argue that, in a disarmed world, states would have no defence if an aggressive personality such as Hitler assumed power and decided to conquer the world. But with general and complete global disarmament a dictator would have no weapons at his disposal. In addition, disarmament should be simply one aspect of a larger plan which involves reorganising the world in such a way that problems such as economic slumps, poverty and social unrest would be eliminated, thus making demagogic dictators less likely. General disarmament would help to remove tension and fear, release valuable natural resources, and free researchers and workers from arms industries to more useful employment.

Talking to each other

The argument that disarmament agreements cannot work has been proven false on several occasions. Sweden and Norway reached what has since proved an extremely successful 'disarmament' agreement when they signed the Karlstad Convention in 1905, following Norway's decision to become totally independent of Sweden. Although Sweden had not been at war for about a hundred years, there were many who thought that the Norwegian decision would spark off a conflict. The Convention saw that it did not. It established a demilitarised zone along the southern frontier, and prohibited concentration of military forces there. A potential war was averted, and Swedish-Norwegian relations became tension-free.

Another classic treaty which worked was the Rush-Bagot Agreement of 1817 between the United States and Britain. At the time both nations were engaged in a bitter and bloody struggle for possession of Canada. A fragile peace had been reached in 1817, but military leaders in Washington and London wanted to maintain and increase their naval strength on the Great Lakes.

Lord Castlereagh, the British foreign secretary, believed any escalation of military strength on the Great Lakes would eventually lead to increased tension and ultimately war. Escalation, he also felt, would prove very costly in the long run, from an economic point of view. The four thousand mile frontier between the United States and Canada was still being drawn up at that time and many areas were disputed. Castlereagh saw that unless quick agreement was reached which could set the pace for other border agreements there was

going to be a lot of trouble. Fortunately, he had the support of a powerful and influential politician in James Monroe, who was to become President in 1817.

Their representatives —Rush and Bagot— negotiated and signed an agreement in 1817, entirely disarming the Great Lakes except for police and customs vessels. Warships on Lake Erie and Lake Ontario were destroyed, and the border between the two North American nations continued to be drawn up in an atmosphere free of tension. G.M. Trevelyan, the British historian, called the solving of the frontier problem 'the greatest operation that has ever been achieved in the interest of peace, and it took many years and many statesmen to accomplish and perfect it.'

The first real move towards large-scale armaments control came at the end of the last century. A number of European nations became involved in an arms race. Several national leaders were worried about the rapid and massive increase in military spending: during the last quarter of the nineteenth century overall military expenditure in the world had increased by about 50 per cent.

Tsar Nicolas II of Russia campaigned for a 'disarmament' conference, which was finally convened at The Hague in 1899. The conference was never intended as a forum to achieve disarmament, but to discuss 'inhumane' weapons and how to slow rising military spending. Although little in the way of pure disarmament emerged, the participants did manage to agree on banning wartime use of dum-dum bullets, which, being made of soft metals, exploded on impact and caused the most frightful wounds. The delegates also adopted a weakly worded communiqué,

'We'll meet again' was almost the only positive message of the 1907 Hague Conference.

to the effect that the limitation of military expenditure was to be greatly desired to help 'the material and moral welfare of humanity.' But there was no mention how limitation would be achieved, and no target date set.

Eight years passed before the Second Hague Conference took place. It soon became clear to the delegates of the 44 nations attending the 1907 conference that during the long interval military budgets had continued to spiral. Not much was achieved at the Conference. Certain norms were set for war on land and sea. The use of poison gas, for example, was outlawed, and limitations placed on aerial warfare. Otherwise, the participating countries were urged in a final communiqué to 'resume the serious examination' of disarmament at a later date. It was agreed to meet again in 1915, but by then World War I had started.

There were no further major disarmament talks until the 1920s, apart from punitive efforts to disarm Germany at the end of World War I. However, in the capitulation agreement forced upon the Germans, it was agreed to consider

steps towards 'the general reduction and limitation' of armed forces and armaments.

The Washington Naval Conference in 1921 was the first real disarmament attempt since the Hague meetings. This gathering was prompted by the fierce naval competition between the United States, Britain and Japan after World War I. The major powers were aware that the 'Dreadnought' warship race between Britain and Germany had created tension prior to World War I, and wanted to avoid a similar race.

The United States, Britain, Japan, Italy and France — the super-powers of the day — participated in the Washington Conference. In many ways the gathering could be considered successful. The negotiating parties, who were under no obligation to discuss 'arms control', nonetheless managed to reach agreement on retaining the status quo so far as battleships and battle cruisers were concerned. Each of the five nations agreed not to build any new battleships or battle cruisers for a ten-year period, to scrap a number of the giant warships, and limit the calibre of guns fitted to vessels such as battleships, aircraft carriers and battle cruisers.

Mussolini   Poincaré   Cecil

The cartoonist Low sums up the discussions in the 1920s: (left) War, the new member of the League of Nations; (right) in the 1930s, another conference fails.

The treaty did not lead to pure disarmament. But it did stabilize, for a time, what was becoming an increasingly tense situation. A follow-up conference was to have taken place in 1932, but it fell apart when France and Italy refused to participate on the grounds that broader disarmament issues should be discussed.

In 1930 a gathering met in London to work out tonnage limitations for smaller warships not covered in the earlier agreement. The United States, Japan and Britain agreed to limitations along the same lines as those applying to the 'Dreadnoughts', and to be extended to cruisers, destroyers and submarines. The French refused to consider the proposal, claiming that because of their colonial undertakings they needed a larger tonnage than Italy. Despite this setback, the meeting did agree to extend the moratorium on the building of new super warships until 1936.

The story of naval disarmament took a sad turn in 1935 when another conference was held in London. With war already in the offing, the gathering was doomed to failure from the start. Japan demanded that every nation be allowed the same number and size of warships, and not higher tonnages for the big powers. The Japanese proposal was rejected, which resulted in Tokyo angrily recalling its delegation and withdrawing from all earlier treaties.

A new naval arms race was set into motion, although the United States, Britain and France agreed between themselves to limit their

battleships to a tonnage of 35,000 tons per vessel, provided that no other country built a warship exceeding that figure. Even Nazi Germany and Russia agreed informally to abide by the agreement. But when word came that Japan was planning a 40,000-ton battleship, the European nations raised their limit to 45,000 tons. That decision brought to an end what were potentially the most successful moves towards disarmament in the inter-war years.

The 1932 Conference

The biggest event during that period was the ill-fated World Disarmament Conference in 1932, convened by the League of Nations. This conference came very close to achieving disarmament. Its preparatory work had started after World War I and the disarmament of Germany — a step generally regarded as a signal for 'general reduction and limitation of armaments' for everyone. When the League of Nations came into being in 1920, one of its first tasks was to set up a special committee to study disarmament. By 1925 a Preparatory Commission had been formed to prepare for a broad conference on disarmament.

Progress was extremely slow, for the task confronting the commission was daunting. No one was sure how to define what was meant by armaments — let alone disarmament. Nonetheless, a rough draft convention was ready by 1930. On 2 February 1932, the World Disarmament Conference got under way under the auspices of the League.

THE CONFERENCE EXCUSES ITSELF

Its preparatory work was immense. The whole spectrum of disarmament had been toothcombed by one committee after another. Decreases in manpower in the armed forces, land, naval and air limitation, the arms trade, chemical warfare and budgetary restrictions had all been thoroughly thrashed out. One observer remarked: 'Whatever other reproaches — and there are many — can be laid at the door of the General Disarmament Conference, that of a lack of preparation is not among them. It resembled nothing so much as an overtrained athlete, who having passed the zenith of fitness, is prone alike to nervous disorder and muscle binding.'

Despite their pulled muscles, the various committees managed to reach a number of compromise solutions on almost all of the issues they had been ordered to discuss. For example, a proposal was put forward, after years of hard work, for reducing military manpower. Amongst other things, it called for the immediate reduction of armed forces to what was termed 'peace time strengths', and it set limits on the amount of time a soldier or an officer might serve. It also proposed that conscription be limited to a maximum of six months' service. Considering the difficulties of implementing such a scheme, the remarkable thing is that all the 58 countries taking part in the disarmament conference agreed in principle to the proposal.

Other procedures were put forward to do away with air forces and reduce and limit military expenditure. Air warfare at that time was regarded in much the same way as nuclear war is regarded today — and with some justification, perhaps, when one remembers the fate of cities such as Rotterdam, Coventry, Dresden, Hamburg and Tokyo, all destroyed during World War II.

Modern treaties

The end of World War II resulted in a new fear of nuclear destruction on a global scale. In 1945 the major powers created a new world body, the United Nations, as a successor to the League. Maintenance of peace was one of the main points in its charter. Shortly after the obliteration of Hiroshima and Nagasaki, the United Nations General Assembly established the Atomic Energy Commission, to act as a watchdog and draw up proposals for limiting nuclear energy and eliminating nuclear weapons. At this stage, there was only one nuclear power — the United States.

A number of plans were then put forward for doing away with the 'Doomsday weapon'. The most notable was the so-called Baruch Plan of 1946. The American initiative called for an international authority under the auspices of the United Nations to control all phases of nuclear energy production and use throughout the world. The authority would also have to have the right of inspection in any of the UN member countries to ensure that no clandestine operations were under way. Many reacted favourably to the plan, but the Soviet Union was opposed to it. It argued that the atom bomb — then possessed only by the U.S. — should be banned first, followed by the gradual destruction of stockpiles. The Russians, although willing to accept a degree of inspection, refused to consider unrestricted inspection. The plan was shelved. As Mr. Baruch put it before making his plan public: 'If we fail, then we have damned every man to be the slave of fear.'

In the 1950s the United Nations abolished its Atomic Energy Commission, and a newly-formed Disarmament Commission was ordered to look at the broad issue of both nuclear and non-nuclear disarmament. In January 1952 the Soviet Union put forward a proposal similar to an American one at the League of Nations Disarmament Conference twenty years earlier. The Soviets called for the major powers to cut their armed forces by a third. The United States rejected the Russian plan, on the grounds that the West would be committed to making bigger cuts than the East under such a scheme. The Americans made a counter-proposal, suggesting that the major powers make proportional cuts, or that maximums be set for the armed forces of the larger nations.

As this debate flowed back and forth, with little progress being made, the Americans lost the nuclear weapon monopoly when the Soviets exploded their first atomic device in 1949. In 1952, the United States exploded their first hydrogen bomb, and the Russians followed suit almost one year later. In 1954, the Russians said they had long-range bombers capable of dropping nuclear bombs upon American cities.

The 1950s saw a whole series of proposals on complete disarmament. France put forward plans in 1952 and 1953, Britain and France jointly suggested a plan in 1954, the Soviet Union came up with a proposal in 1954, the United States followed suit in 1955, the Russians retaliated with a new one in 1959 — and so on. There was little disagreement over what was needed to be done. Most countries agreed that the force levels of the nuclear powers would have to be limited to a fixed rate, and that nuclear weapons should be totally prohibited. The main problem, which still remains, was verification — general

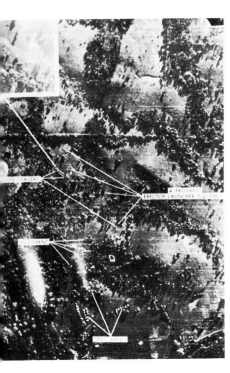

Cuba 1962: Perhaps the nearest the world has yet got to nuclear war. Photographic evidence of missile sites and cartoon comment on the confrontation.

principles of control and inspection to make sure that everyone sticks to the agreement.

Hopes soared in 1960 — a ten-nation East-West disarmament committee was formed. But one year later came the withdrawl of the five Warsaw Pact countries. They maintained that the West was not serious about achieving disarmament, but only interested in partial measures. Finally, however, the countries agreed to return, and the so-called 18-nation Geneva Disarmament Conference started in the winter of 1961. Unfortunately, France immediately withdrew, believing it was not getting enough say.

Although 31 nations are now represented at the Geneva Disarmament Conference, little progress has resulted. There have been a whole series of 'limited' disarmament or control measures taken on a multilateral and bilateral basis, involving Washington and Moscow. The first agreement successfully negotiated was the Antarctic Treaty, signed in 1959 by twelve nations, including the USA, the USSR, France and Britain, declaring that the Antarctic could be used only for peaceful purposes. Nuclear energy, either in the form of weapons or energy, was also outlawed in the Antarctic. A similar pact was signed in 1967, banning military activity in outer space.

But both of these treaties only banned weapons from areas where there was scant military interest anyway. As the Stockholm International Peace Research Institute put it: 'Who wants to conduct military manoeuvres on the moon or establish a military base on Venus?'

The 1967 Treaty of Tlatelolco, aimed at making Latin America a nuclear free zone, was another toothless wonder. The only Latin nations with the capacity and resources to make nuclear weapons are Brazil and Argentina, and these two countries — not the best of friends — have refused to sign the document.

Even the widely acclaimed 1963 Partial Test Ban Treaty is open to serious criticism. It took 64 months to hammer out, and bans all nuclear tests in the atmosphere, under the water and in outer space. But it allows nations to carry out underground tests, and can be regarded more as an anti-pollution measure rather than a step towards disarmament. It did not even limit actual testing. As a result, the United States, the Soviet Union and Britain have carried out the same number of tests, on average, as they did before the treaty was signed. By 1975 over a thousand nuclear explosions had been conducted since World War II.

Perhaps the most important treaty reached during the 1960s was the Nuclear Non-Proliferation Treaty (NPT), signed in 1968 after seven years of intensive debate. This agreement prohibits nuclear countries with nuclear weapons from transferring nuclear weapons or other nuclear devices to anyone else. It also bans non-nuclear states who have signed the treaty from acquiring the weapons.

However, many feel that the current NPT treaty is too weak in the light of the current interest among small states in nuclear power as a source of energy. Many countries seem prepared to consider nuclear energy, despite its problems, such as disposal of radio-active waste. Another danger is that a byproduct of nuclear reactors is plutonium, which is usable for the production of nuclear weapons.

The Nuclear Non-Proliferation Treaty aimed at stopping the emergence of a sixth nuclear power. It failed. In 1974 India exploded a nuclear device. Unless the MPT treaty is strengthened, the world will find itself with even more nuclear nations. Another major problem is that the treaty does nothing to stop the 'haves' from increasing their arsenals.

The 1970s, designated the decade of disarmament by the United Nations, has seen two major multilateral 'arms control' agreements. A 1971 convention prohibited the placing of nuclear weapons and other mass destruction weapons on the sea bed and ocean floor. The following year, another convention banned the development, production and stockpiling of bacteriological or biological and toxic weapons, and required the destruction of existing stocks. This treaty bans germ warfare, and came into force in 1975. It is one of the few in the last twenty-five years to contain any real disarmament measures, though it should be realized that military establishments view biological warfare as technically unfeasible.

In addition to the multilateral treaties, the two super-powers have signed several bilateral agreements. The 'Hot Line' telephone link between Washington and Moscow was established in 1963. In times of high tension Washington and Moscow can discuss their intentions, hoping thus to avoid or explain the accidental use of nuclear weapons. The hot line was set up in the wake of the Cuban missile crisis, when President Kennedy threatened to unleash the United States nuclear missiles on the Soviet Union unless the Russians ceased delivery of missiles to Cuba. It has been used during various Middle East wars and other crises.

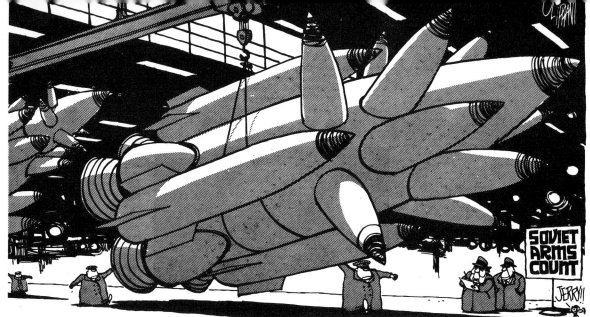

'One . . .   / Olipnant © 1975 Washington Star

Other agreements between the two powers include a 1971 treaty to reduce the risks of accidental nuclear war. This calls for the immediate notification by the other nation in the event of an accidental, unauthorized event involving the possible detonation of a nuclear weapon, and immediate notification in the event of missile-warning systems picking up unidentified objects.

In 1973 an agreement was reached between the United States and the Soviet Union aimed at preventing incidents on, or over, the high seas. In 1974 they limited underground nuclear tests and prohibited tests which exceed a yield of 150 kilotons — the equivalent of 150,000 tons of TNT. Yet the vast majority of underground tests carried out by the two super-powers are already well within this limit: the agreement represents no serious brake on the arms race.

Russo-American talks on strategic arms limitations have dominated the spotlight recently. They started in 1969, and by 1972 the two powers had agreed to restrict anti-ballistic missiles to defence of the international capitals, plus one area where intercontinental ballistic missiles are deployed. Another agreement also 'froze' until 1977 the total number of fixed land-based ICBM launchers and submarine-launched ballistic missiles.

Although the strategic arms limitation talks may have temporarily halted the spread of certain types of missiles, they have done nothing to stop qualitative improvements. For example, there are no restrictions upon the number of warheads packed into an ICBM missile. It comes as no surprise to discover that the Americans and Russians are developing new missiles that can carry more and bigger warheads.

One step forward, two steps back

The last thirty years have seen the active involvement of thousands of people in the disarmament field. At one conference after another they have discussed plans for arms control, disarmament proposals, nuclear free zones and 'peace' zones. In Europe alone, there have been proposals for the disengagement and withdrawal of the great powers from certain areas, to create European nuclear-free zones, and to inspect against surprise attack. Elsewhere, there have been proposals to denuclearize Africa, to register and publicize all imports and exports of conventional weapons, ammunition and implements of war, and to create a peace zone in the Indian Ocean.

But for every one person working for disarmament, thousands more are working or

'Don't despair; the others might be easier!'

contributing to the arms race. The history of disarmament over the past thirty years has been a case of one step forward, two steps back. The public has been misled by the optimism surrounding each new agreement. Where have all the doves gone? While politicians talk disarmament, the military stuff arsenals. Despite the euphoric statements emanating from Moscow and Washington, the world has not yet seen any real move towards 'general and complete disarmament.'

The United Nations Secretary General said in 1970 that if we are to progress towards disarmament, 'governments must approach this subject in a new spirit. They must stop questioning the seriousness of purpose of others and think how they can demonstrate their own.'

As American researcher John G. Stoessinger has put it: 'While aggression may be inherent in us all, war is learned behaviour and, as such, can

be unlearned, and, ultimately, selected out entirely. There have been other habits of mankind that seemed impossible to shed. In the Ice Age, when people lived in caves, incest was perfectly acceptable. No one except mother and sister was around. Today, incest is virtually gone. Cannibalism provides an even more dramatic case. Thousands of years ago, human beings ate each other and drank each other's blood. That, too, was part of 'human nature.' Even a brief century ago, millions of Americans believed that God had ordained white people to be free and black people to be slaves. Why else would He have created them in different colours? Yet slavery, once a part of 'human nature', was abolished because human beings showed a capacity for growth. The growth came slowly, after immense suffering, but it *did* come. Human nature had been changed. Like slavery and cannibalism, war too can be eliminated from mankind's arsenal of horrors.'

Answers to aggression

Protection for the civilian

Digging in. An underground World War Two shelter provides escape from gas attack and bomb blast.

Stairs will give some protection against falling debris. Advice for a nuclear attack from a British government booklet first published in 1957.

If you are trapped inside your air raid shelter and the air outside is full of radioactive fallout this is how you are supposed to filter the air. From a Russian civil defence handbook.

L'abri ne peut assurer la survie que s'il remplit certaines conditions... Il doit:

être hermétiquement isolé

contre les effets des toxiques de combat, des armes biologiques et des retombées radioactives.

protéger

contre la chaleur et les rayonnements radioactifs.

Pendant la guerre de 1939–1945 on pouvait vivre au maximum quelques heures dans les abris. Aujourd'hui, ils doivent être organisés de manière à rendre la vie possible pendant plusieurs jours. Les radiations atomiques peuvent développer leurs effets mortels pendant des semaines.
L'abri doit être équipé pour accueillir instantanément ses occupants. La vie doit pouvoir se poursuivre dans la sécurité même si le danger se prolonge.
L'abri permettra certains travaux; on ne le quittera que par force majeure tant que la menace demeure suspendue à l'extérieur.

rendre la vie possible

par le renouvellement et le filtrage de l'air, par réserves de et d'eau (voir page 3

résister

au poids des décombres ainsi qu'à l'onde de choc des bombes brisantes ou atomiques.

pouvoir quitter l'abri

par voies d'évacuation et sorties de secours.

L'abri doit donc être bien enterré! Il comprendra une voie d'évacuation couverte d'une dalle à l'épreuve du poids des décombres et des sorties de secours situées

A double page spread from 'Defense civile', a 300 page book given free to every household in Switzerland, with information on how to survive the next war, whether of the guerrilla or atomic kind.

Every home should have one. A steel and concrete fallout shelter for a family of six, on sale in Hamburg.

6 NO MORE UNTO THE BREACH

'Would you tell me, please, which way I ought to go from here?'
'That depends a good deal on where you want to get to,' said the Cat.
'I don't much care where,' said Alice.
'Then it doesn't matter which way you go,' said the Cat.

Lewis Carroll, *Alice in Wonderland*

Israeli paratroopers are handed rifle and Bible to mark the end of their training.

Vietnam, 1968.

Global disarmament has been sought for hundreds of years. One proposal after another has been put forward for bringing permanent peace to our troubled planet. But disarmament is unlikely to be achieved until drastic surgery is performed on the international system.

The United Nations sadly represents the latest failure to bring about such a system. Nonetheless, there are steps that leading governments can initiate which would point in the direction of a less perilous world.

A commitment to disarmament can be demonstrated by establishing a new organisation to replace the United Nations Disarmament Conference in Geneva, which has achieved next to nothing. A new disarmament organisation, which represents more nations and coordinates all disarmament efforts, might provide fresh impetus for peace talks.

Fear of suspected technological military advances or arms buildups in an enemy country is a major factor when a nation decides to step up arms production. This fear of the unknown could be alleviated by the establishment of a United Nations agency, which would collect and disseminate information on national armaments, and make certain that governments adhered to disarmament agreements.

The nuclear countries can easily demonstrate a willingness to move towards disarmament by immediately freezing their atomic armaments at current levels; these nations already have the capacity to kill every human being on the planet. A freeze in the nuclear arms race would open the door for realistic negotiations to slowly decrease stockpiles.

With arms exports running into billions of dollars it is all too obvious that the powerful economic forces of the nuclear powers would not look kindly upon a slackening in arms development, research and production. The task for peace workers, therefore, is to put to rest the old bogey that military expenditure is vital for national health, to show that the economic dislocation caused by the closure of arms industries would not prove insurmountable.

A disarmament group at the International Peace Research Association in Norway believes the public has been put to sleep as a result of the 'cosmetics' of so-called disarmament negotiations and 'tunes of detente.' The group, which includes researchers from East and West, has called for a concerted international effort to revive the disarmament movement. These are some of the steps they suggest need to be taken:

- Any strategy for disarmament must start by ferreting out and examining within each nation the forces blocking disarmament.

- From this base, the disarmament movement would become a global force, because of the interlocking nature of the world economy.

- Total disarmament must be pursued by means of fixed schedules, procedures, ways and means. Talks should focus on real limitations and cutbacks of destructive capabilities.

- Military research and development must be limited and reduced. The public should be informed of the potential benefits of military efforts being directed towards peaceful purposes.

- There must be a prohibition on nuclear weapons, and a destruction of all stockpiles.

- This requires a comprehensive nuclear test ban treaty, which would prohibit testing, and include an agreement on 'no first use' of nuclear weapons. This should be followed by a general outlawing of nuclear weapons, and a reduction in and eventual elimination of delivery systems for nuclear warheads.

- There would need to be tighter control of the transfer of nuclear materials, while the technology for the peaceful use of nuclear energy should be made available to non-nuclear states.

- Effective disarmament must take conventional weapons into account. Weapons such as fragmentation bombs and napalm should be banned, as should the development, production and stockpiling of all chemical weapons.

- There should be a code to govern the world arms trade, and measures to establish international control of sales and transfers.

- The secrecy surrounding armaments, a major cause of tension between nations, must be ended.

In our nuclear-minded world, nations are already finding alternatives to battlefields. In 1973 oil-producing nations used the threat of an oil embargo to achieve better prices for petroleum.

There is a parallel between workers organizing themselves into trade unions to achieve economic justice, and smaller nations organizing themselves to confront the major powers with demands for a fairer distribution of wealth.

In the words of Sean MacBride as he accepted the Nobel Peace prize, grossly unfair economic conditions, which still condemn most human beings to starvation, disease and poverty, 'constitute in themselves aggression against their victims'.

Campaigns or conferences?

CND on the march.

Buddhist monks outside the Aldershot Arms Fair.

Nato heads in conference.

Acknowledgements

The board of the Stockholm International Peace Research Institute (SIPRI) deserves a special word of thanks for providing financial backing for this book, along with the unstinting assistance of its researchers and the full run of the Institute's extensive library. May I also thank Randy Forsberg, who during her time at SIPRI assisted me immeasurably, and all my other friends who provided advice and moral support. The daunting task of editing this manuscript fell upon Roger Choate. His expertise was invaluable.

Illustration acknowledgements

Camera Press: 10/11 bot, 21, 32 top, 33, 34, 35, 42 rt, 43 rt, 44/45, 48 top, 50, 51, 58, 72 top, 73, 77, 90, 95 top/bot; Imperial War Museum: 4, 18 bot/rt, 25, 42 lft, 47; Sunday Times: 14, 27, 30 bot, 31; Andrew de Lory: 2; John Hillelson Agency: Don McCullin 3, Cornell Capa/Magnum 28/29, J P Lafon 36, Tony Koroda/Sygma 39 top, 62/63, Alan Nogues/Sygma 68, 69, Salheim/Sygma 72 bot, Simon Pietri/Sygma 85; David Alexander Simpson: 5, Keystone Press: 6, 83 lft, 89 bot; Ron Chapman: 7; Times Newspaper: 8 top; Robert Haas: 8 bot; Hector Breeze/Private Eye: 9 top; Nato Photo: 11 top; Sawyer Press: 12; René Burri: 13; Unesco Courier: 15 top; Ian Berry/Magnum 17; The Associated Press: 26, 27 top, 43 lft, 75 bot/centre; Crown Copyright/Central Office 30; Scientific American 32 bot; United Press International 38; British Film Institute 48; Daily Mirror 51 top; Sanity: Herblock 17; Observer: 55; Albert/Punch 57; Los Angeles Times: 59; Chicago Sun Times: 60; Cassell and Collier Macmillan: 65; Chris Schwartz: 68 bot; Mary Evans Picture Library: 74, 79; Popperphoto: 75; Low/Evening Standard: 80, 81; Daily Express 83 rt; Newsweek: 86/87; Pressens Bild Stockholm: 91; A Martin/New Yorker: 93; Euan Duff: 94 top; Topix: 94 bot.

Bibliography

In order to research and write this book, I have referred to and read many other books dealing with war and peace, (Library shelves are filled with books on war). I leaned heavily upon the following books, among many others:

Geoffrey Blainey, *The Causes of War*, MacMillan, 1973.

Nigel Calder (ed.), *Unless Peace Comes*, Allen Lane, 1968.

William Epstein, *Disarmament — 25 Years of Effort*, Canadian Institute of International Affairs, 1971.

J.F.C. Fuller, *The Decisive Battles of the Western World 480 B.C.-1757*, Paladin, 1972.

S. Glasstone (ed.), *The Effects of Nuclear Weapons*, United States Atomic Energy Commission, 1964.

Philip Noel-Baker, *The Arms Race*, Calder, 1958.

Red Cross, *Weapons that may cause unnecessary suffering or have indiscriminate effects*, International Committee of the Red Cross, Geneva, 1973.

Nicholas Sims, *Approaches to Disarmament*, Society of Friends of Peace and International Relations Committee, 1974.

Stockholm International Peace Research Institute, *World Armament and Disarmament SIPRI Yearbook 1974*, Almqvist & Wiksell, Stockholm, 1974.

Stockholm International Peace Research Institute, *World Armament and Disarmament SIPRI Yearbook 1975*, Almqvist & Wiksell, Stockholm, 1975.

John Stoessinger, *Why nations go to war?*, St Martins Press, New York, 1974.

United Nations Organization, *Economic and Social Consequences of Disarmament*, UNO, New York, 1962.

Donald A. Wells, *The War Myth*, Pegasus, New York, 1974.